CHOiCES

DECIDING RIGHT AND WRONG TODAY

CHOiCES
DECIDING RIGHT AND WRONG TODAY

Margaret Killingray

Published by
BRF
Elsfield Hall, 15–17 Elsfield Way
Oxford OX2 8EP
ISBN 1 84101 194 0

First published 2001
10 9 8 7 6 5 4 3 2 1 0
All rights reserved

Acknowledgments
Unless otherwise stated, scripture quotations taken from the *Holy Bible,
New International Version*, copyright © 1973, 1978, 1984 by
International Bible Society, are used by permission of Hodder &
Stoughton Limited. All rights reserved. 'NIV' is a registered trademark
of International Bible Society. UK trademark number 1448790.

Scriptures quoted from the Good News Bible published by The Bible
Societies/HarperCollins Publishers Ltd, UK © American Bible Society
1966, 1971, 1976, 1992, used with permission.

Scriptures quoted from the New Jerusalem Bible, published and
copyright © 1985 by Darton, Longman and Todd Ltd and les Editions
du Cerf, and by Doubleday, a division of Bantam Doubleday Dell
Publishing Group, Inc. Used by permission of Darton, Longman and
Todd Ltd, and Doubleday, a division of Random House, Inc.

A catalogue record for this book is available from the British Library

Printed and bound in Great Britain by
Omnia Books Limited, Glasgow

Foreword

If the 1960s were an era of moral libertarianism, our own time is becoming an age of moral anxiety. Society followed the lead of the radicals who proclaimed that 'doing your own thing' would lead to personal fulfilment and a happier life for all. Nobody told us that the price of individualism is the loss of community, the collapse of respect between generations, and the increasing fragility of the marriage bond.

Intoxicated with a new freedom from moral constraints, society at first turned its back on the more disturbing, even destructive implications of everyone doing what was right in their own eyes, but the 1990s saw a steadily increasing sense of moral disquiet. Secular commentators and leading politicians joined in expressing concern that things might already have gone too far. Some feared that we were lurching towards a moral anarchy, in which some children seemed close to losing any sense of right and wrong.

Like the last days of the Roman Empire, when a dying civilization collapsed into the self-destructive excesses of casual sex, narcissism and excessive consumption of food and drink, the new millennium may yet be characterized by a riot of self-indulgence that signals the last days of the West. We no longer make careful moral choices, informed by an agreed code of conduct: we do whatever we happen to feel like, with the priorities of 'me first', 'instant gratification', and 'to hell with the consequences'.

Most people have friends or family members who have become victims of such impulsive selfishness. Those who provide any kind of counselling constantly encounter the impact of selfish and inconsiderate living in damaged and broken lives. John Donne was right to say that no one is an island: we are all both sinned against and sinning and the consequences of our moral decisions are mapped out in the lives of others. The more we 'do our own thing', the more we become the victims, however unintentional at times, of the 'own thing' done by others.

Faced with a moral vacuum, some are attracted to authoritarian leaders who declaim what is right and wrong in every conceivable circumstance and detail of life. Ethical fundamentalism can be found in every religious setting, from the orthodox Jews in Jerusalem who throw stones at a woman in a mini-skirt, to the Islamic Taliban of Afghanistan who exclude women from education and employment, to the American Christian anti-abortionists who fire-bombed an abortion clinic to affirm their dedication to the sanctity of life. In reaction against moral anarchy, such groups look for a moral absolutism, in which there is never any room for any shade of grey.

Margaret Killingray scrupulously avoids such simplistic and crude excesses. She explores the many different influences that shape our moral thinking, including our family background, our social and national setting, our temperament and our gender. Through the stories of many individuals' moral crises, well chosen and vividly told, she reveals the difficulty of moral decision-making in the real world. And then she demonstrates just how helpful the Bible continues to be in providing an ethical framework that allows us to make the most of life. I was particularly grateful for her emphasis on the church as a faith community in which we have the opportunity—often neglected or even forgotten—to support one another, exploring and discovering the practical implications of biblical teaching for our daily ethical choices.

Repulsed by extremism, many in the West are looking for a new approach to ethics that recovers the distinction between right and wrong but is realistic about the conflicting priorities and painful consequences that are likely to result from many real-life moral choices. Between the anarchists and the ayatollahs—between doing your own thing and always having a pre-packaged answer to every moral dilemma—Margaret Killingray demonstrates a third way. Those who have lost confidence in the legitimacy of any moral absolutes will see how biblical values really can make sense of life. Those who have been over-judgmental will see anew the complexity of real-life decision making. This book provides a clear and practical route map to ethics in the real world.

Margaret Killingray not only has a professional understanding of the issues of theoretical ethics, she also has a very clear and sympathetic grasp of what makes life tick for ordinary people. You may not agree with all her conclusions, but *Choices* will help you to choose wisely and live well. I warmly commend this book, which is full of practical wisdom for making the most of life.

Rob Warner

Contents

PART ONE

The way we live now

Chapter 1

Muddling along

John and Peg are having a conservatory put on to the back of their house. Images of lovely spring evenings, sitting in the glow of the sunset, warm and comfortable after a busy day, fill them both with great pleasure. On their own with all their children gone, the planning and choosing of carpets, furniture and curtains make up for the slightly empty feel of a house that was once full of growing young people. The hassle of finding builders is over; the estimate is reasonable.

One morning, the man in charge mentions to John that he would like to be paid in cash; it is apparent that he will not be paying income tax and is offering to avoid adding value-added tax to the bill. He is being generous and helpful to John and Peg as well as to himself.

Later that evening, John and Peg talk about the builder's request and wonder how they should respond. While they are talking, there is the sound of a key in the lock, and their youngest daughter walks in. She looks round at the nearly finished room, at the catalogues and curtain samples. She asks them why on earth they are spending so much money on themselves when there are empty bedrooms upstairs, homeless people on the streets, and beyond that a hungry and suffering world.

John and Peg were taken by surprise, caught off-balance by a builder they were employing, and a daughter they had brought up. Each presented them with issues they had not even thought about, questions they had never asked. Of course they knew that there were a hundred ways of not being quite straight in business dealings, and of course they knew that some people spent large amounts of money on high living and never gave to needy causes. But on the whole they assumed, without thinking about it very much, that other people did those things and not them. Their immediate response to the builder was that only the government was losing out, that no person was being hurt, and that if they refused to pay him cash they would be throwing his generous offer back in his face and making life difficult for themselves. They were a little affronted by a daughter's criticism when they remembered some of the trials she had put them through when she was growing up.

Like many of us, they could see the general principles but found it hard to see how to apply them in particular circumstances. They could believe that cheating, stealing and self-indulgence were wrong, and that generosity and fair play were right. But they were very unsure what those high-sounding moral values meant when it came to making decisions about their conservatory. Surely rules were meant to be bent, especially when it would be very difficult and embarrassing not to do so.

How would we respond to challenges like this? If we look back on our lives, how have we solved such problems? Perhaps at the time we were not even aware that we had made a decision. Many of us may not be too pleased with ourselves when we look back at some of the actions we have taken and the way we have behaved. In ordinary everyday living, we are glad that others cannot know about some of the things we have done.

There can be very few of us who have always behaved exactly as we would have liked. If we had had time to think, or could have seen the issues more clearly in the first place, things might have worked out better. We often speak and act before we think. We are sometimes blinded by anger or love. Most of us are not consistent, are not quite sure what the rights and wrongs are, when faced with a problem that has to be dealt with on the spot. Is it possible to be more prepared, to have a greater understanding of ourselves, other people and the world in which we live? Is it possible to learn how to make the right decisions and to do so more often? How can we find out what the right decisions are? In other words, how can we learn the best way to live?

In our heads there are a range of guidelines and rules. Some come from our upbringing, our parents and our schools; some come from the groups that we belong to, some from religious sources, some from television and the media. Some we keep; some we don't. Some we keep one day, because we feel like it, and not another day because we feel mean and lousy. Most of us can harbour two contradictory rules at the same time—rather like making the Christmas pudding, muttering, 'Too many cooks spoil the broth' and 'Many hands make light work' at the same time.

Sometimes our problems with knowing what is wrong and what is right arise because our world is changing so fast that we are constantly facing new situations that do not fit into our existing ways of thinking. My husband's grandmother was a fierce old lady, with very strong views about right and wrong. These included hair length and whether shirts should be tucked into trousers. She spoke darkly about the evils of dancing, theatre, films and the cinema. When she was in her eighties, she moved to live with my mother-in-law and for the first time sat in a room with a television. She accepted it completely, watching everything that came on—sitcoms, fashion, pop programmes, cartoons, 'Come Dancing'. She never said anything against it. It was something new. Her ideas about what was evil were already fixed and she could not see that television was similar to theatre and cinema. This made for a more peaceful house, but it highlights one of the problems we all face. When times change, we don't always apply old rules to new situations.

This book is in two parts. In the first part we will look at the way most of us make decisions about right and wrong. We will ask why people act in the way they do; whether there are rules of right and wrong that are the same for all human beings; whether there are other rules that only apply to certain groups and are, perhaps, only British, or only male, or only for the rich. We will ask how far individual ideas of right and wrong arise because of individual differences—whether someone is fussy or very happy-go-lucky, depressed or on top of the world.

Why do we sometimes not do what we know is right, and sometimes make a mess of our own lives, even though everyone else around us warned us it would happen? The answers to these questions can help us to be wiser and more understanding about ourselves and others.

This first section will also look at our world and ask what are the strongest influences on us that might be making our ideas of right and wrong change. In particular we will look at relationships, living with other people, and see how these are changing. Some of the greatest changes are happening in our ideas of what is right in our marriages, families and friendships.

In the second section, we will ask whether there is a Christian way to live that is different from any other way. If there is, how do we find out about it? If we become a Christian, what kind of changes might we have to make to the way we think about morals and values? This will mean looking at how the Christian Church has taught about right and wrong in the past, and also at how we can use the Bible as a guide for living.

Some of you may wonder whether there is anything individuals can do to influence the way our societies and communities are changing. I believe that there is. We can, first of all, be more aware of ourselves and our fellows and have more understanding of the world around us and how it functions.

Most of us do respond to the opinions of others, especially those we love and admire. In that way we may have some influence on our own circles of family, friends and colleagues. I believe that living as a Christian is the way to discover how to live a good life. There are, of course, large numbers of people who live good and creative lives who are not Christians, and Christians who do not. But in a changing world, many are searching for a firm base for living, and are finding it increasingly difficult to keep to the patterns they think are right when such patterns are being challenged. Being a disciple of Jesus Christ does provide that firm base.

At certain points throughout the book I want to focus on one particular activity, and that is parenting. If there is any point at which we can make some changes in how the world is developing, it is at the point where adults, and not just parents, have the care, nurture and education of children in their hands. Children learn how to handle the world at a very early age and much of what they learn comes from the adults round them—not so much from what they say, but from what they do, how they act and the kind of people they are.

Some people reading this book may not be Christians. You will find that much in the first section is relevant to anyone who lives in a 'western' society. The main patterns of ethical thinking in modern Europe and North America, as well as some other parts of the world, all stem from a combination of classic Greek thinking, medieval Catholicism, the Reformation and what we call the Enlightenment, which is the word used for some of the new ways of thinking about human life that arose as the Industrial Revolution changed Europe. We need to add to those some powerful ideas that came with the new thinking in psychology, sociology and economics, science and tech- nology, over the past hundred or so years.

Those who are from other parts of the world, particularly from Asia, have inherited the ethics of other great systems of human thought—Buddhism, Hinduism and Islam, among others—although all these ways of thinking about right and wrong have much in common. They all rub shoulders with each other in the modern world. They influence each other and sometimes are mixed together. In the countries of Western Europe all these ways of thinking came together as people moved from other parts of the world to Europe, bringing their own ways and cultures, as well as religions, with them. In the same way, Europeans went out to other parts of the world, taking European ways of thinking with them, and sometimes setting up European-style schools that again brought different ways of thinking into contact and collision. Christians are having to think afresh about their own ways of acting and thinking as the world round them changes, and to ask whether sometimes they have mistaken their own culture's ways, whether they are British, or American, or middle-class, or white, for the Christian way. Much of this change and adaptation is uncomfortable, particularly for older generations. This book sets out to bring some understanding and a wider vision to take us into the next 1000 years!

CHAPTER 2

Living by the rules

John and Peg, the couple building their conservatory, were faced by two dilemmas. The first was whether they should accept their builder's offer to cut the price by paying neither income nor sales tax. The second was whether they should have spent the money on themselves anyway. When they sat down to think about these issues, they might have asked themselves whether there were rules to guide them.

We are using the word 'rule' here in a very broad sense. It is rather like the way in which we call an accurate measure of length a 'ruler' or 'rule', but we also sometimes use the phrase 'rule of thumb' for a more rough and ready measurement. Take a very general traditional saying such as 'It is better to be safe than sorry'. This may simply be something the grandfather says when he straps the toddler into her high chair against her wishes. But it could be an important rule when we are tempted to jump a red light. And 'better safe than sorry' may not be a very good guide if we are standing on the edge of an icy pond into which a child has fallen. Whose safety and whose sorrow are we talking about?

We could use a whole range of other words—principles, values, guidelines, instructions or laws, or even feelings of distaste might be included. All of these words have slightly different meanings. But we can see how, in any situation, some guidance under all, or at least some, of these headings may be jostling for attention inside our heads. Buried deep down in our personalities there may be rules that we are not aware of, making us act in one way rather than another.

One kind of rule comes in the form of laws made by the government, which we can be forced to keep by the threat of arrest and punishment if we do not. In John and Peg's relationship with their builder, these kinds of rules are being broken. He is bound by law to be taxed on the money he earns and they have to pay value-added tax on the money they pay him. They are breaking the law if they do not. However, other kinds of rules that are not legal rules on the statute book are in operation at the same time.

Most people think that stealing is wrong and that there should be a rule against it. Many would probably regard what the builder and our couple were contemplating as stealing. However, many people do not think that all forms of stealing are as bad as each other: they may agree with John and Peg that rules of courtesy and neighbourliness are just as important and that they should not embarrass someone by refusing a generous offer. Also, many would say that John and Peg should look after themselves, that there are 'rules' of self-interest, that money does not grow on trees, so they should pay as little as they can, as long as they were not hurting or cheating the builder too much.

For many people today, rules about being kind and helpful sound much more attractive and much more convincing than the more official ones that the government has made. But John and Peg's daughter is challenging them to keep these rules about being kind and helpful. She is telling them that they are being mean, keeping everything for themselves, not being generous. They do not take much notice of what she says because she is their daughter. She is not someone who has authority to tell them what to do. If anything, they may think she should be listening to them—something she may not have done very often in the past.

For many of us, the most important place where we have to decide how to speak and act is in our own homes, in our personal relationships. But the rules here are not written up on the kitchen wall for us to refer to. One family I knew did have a list on the kitchen wall of activities like tidying up the toys, doing homework and going to bed on time, and the children won silver stars when they had done them. For most of us, the rules and guidelines for family living are much more vague. Being considerate may mean cleaning the bath after use, but it also means a range of attitudes and behaviour which are far more difficult to specify.

John and Peg cannot hear what their daughter is saying because of their resentment that she should criticize them. But later they may think again about what she has said. There is a challenge there. Perhaps they will decide to see if there are any students at the local college who need accommodation. They may decide to give some money away to a charity that happens to send them an appeal in the post at the right moment.

Somewhere in our heads, as part of the complicated processes and memories that make up a human being, we are all possessors of a large number of different kinds of rules and regulations. Some have great force, such as the law that murder is wrong, which we would probably regard as very important even if it were not the law of the land. Others matter very little to us, like the posting dates for Christmas mail. Such a 'rule' as that is not about right and wrong. However, some people who are very conscious of rules and regulations can become worried and even guilty if they post their letters a day late! Some rules we all keep, more or less. The percentage of those wearing passenger seatbelts went from about half to almost one hundred per cent overnight when it became law in Britain. We are not so good about keeping to speed limits!

Some rules have a very long history and we have known them all our lives. Sometimes we are confronted with new rules, perhaps made up yesterday by our headteacher or our boss. In general, however, we are not aware of where all the rules that we have in our heads come from. Perhaps the best way to understand this is to imagine that we are one particular person and to construct the many different ways one person would think—the rules they would recall—in all the many different situations of everyday life.

Mary is a 34-year-old woman. She is married with three children. She is a doctor who works part-time in a local surgery. She lives in a London suburb. She is ethnically Indian, her parents having come to the UK from Kerala in South India when she was three years old. She is a Christian, like her parents, and she sometimes goes to a local Baptist church.

Some rules are common to all cultures, and Mary is going to be like most other people in the world in some of the rules she tries to keep, such as doing her very best to care for her children and trying to keep the rules of the country she is living in. Like many people, she may believe it is important to make her children do their homework and clean their teeth.

Some rules come from being a member of certain kinds of groups, and in those ways she is going to be like some, but not all, other people.

She will care for her patients in similar ways to doctors all over the world. But she may believe that being Christian means that there are rules for her to obey that others do not, like going to church and praying.

There may also be some rules that are important to her because she is a certain kind of person. She may be very tidy, and want all her family to be tidy too. Of course, there are lots of tidy people in the world, who think that tidiness is an important moral virtue, but it is not because they are women, or doctors, or mothers, or come from an ethnic minority, but simply because of the way they have developed as an individual.

Suppose we watch Mary through one day. What situations does she meet and what rules and guidelines, principles and values guide her?

In the morning, around 7am, one child complains that he has a tummy ache and doesn't want to go to school. Mary has to decide very quickly whether he is exaggerating or pretending, in which case she should encourage him to get up and get going, or whether he is really ill and should be allowed to stay in bed. If she is wrong either way, she may be in for a difficult day and will feel very guilty at the end of it. Compulsory schooling and the importance of good attendance, good doctoring of her own child, loving mothering and parental discipline all play their part in her decision.

At breakfast she shouts at her husband because he gets up to go to work without clearing the dishes. But Mary has been brought up in such a way that she feels she should not be angry, and should not lose her temper and shout. She believes there should be communication and understanding between marriage partners. Mary also fights against a feeling that comes from her upbringing that men should not do women's jobs.

She drives her children to school and goes on to work. There are a lot of rules about driving and many conventions about behaviour behind the wheel of a car. Mary may feel guilty about using her car in a very busy city, adding to the congestion and the pollution.

In the surgery she sees another doctor's patients and is required to give sleeping pills to someone, against her better judgment. She has to deal with a tearful young woman who wants an abortion. Rules that come from her beliefs as a Christian, from her knowledge of what is best for patients, from her sympathetic understanding as a woman, and from her duty to the practice that employs her, all fight their way into her decision-making.

After work she goes shopping. A headache clouds her thinking. She has to decide what the family are going to eat that evening, and rules about what are good eating habits battle with issues of ease and convenience. Mary is also keen to do her part to fight some of the evils in the world by buying goods that are fairly traded. She needs to search for certain kinds of coffee. She would like to buy cane sugar and not beet sugar, but she is too tired to bother. At the checkout the middle-aged woman in the queue behind her tries to help her with the process of checking out, speaking slowly and deliberately in simple English. Now Mary briefly loses her identity as a working professional woman, because she has been identified as someone from a minority group who probably cannot manage simple tasks like shopping and who probably cannot speak English very well. She bites back the temptation to respond with an angry and clever reply and goes home.

Mary is a parent, and her early morning problem of a child who does not want to go to school, or who just may be ill, is one that many parents have known, but in the past she has faced more difficult and long-term problems.

When Mary's first child was born, she was working full-time. Her husband Stephan is a research scientist. They had good full-time childcare arranged and both planned to continue their careers. However, Jamie was born with serious feeding difficulties and as Mary's maternity leave came to an end they realized that it was not going to be possible to put him into paid care for at least another six months. Neither Mary nor Stephan could face giving up work, and the arguments became very bitter. Commitment to their child and to each other, and questions about whose priorities were the more important, who was earning more, who could afford to lose time out of a career and whether his mother or his father was the best person to look after Jamie, were all part of the argument. Decisions that had been far more straightforward for past generations were a new source of strain for these modern parents.

Mary and Stephan have many choices, even though some of them might be difficult to make. For some, the *lack* of choices can make it difficult to lead a morally responsible life. On a television newsreel several years ago, a young mother was caught on camera, holding her small son, watching the joyriders smash stolen cars as they drove them spectacularly up and down in front of her block of flats. Someone asked her why she was there. 'It's something to watch that's exciting. There isn't anything else to do,' she replied. 'But the cars are stolen,' the interviewer said. 'Why should I care?' she replied. 'I haven't got a car.'

In the next chapters, we look in more detail at where our rules and values come from and how we acquire them.

CHAPTER 3

Where do all the rules come from?

If I landed on Mars and was surrounded by a crowd of very strange aliens, I would be overjoyed to see another human being, even if it was someone from the other side of the world, with no common language. What we had in common, as humans from the same planet, would make us feel like sisters. We would know that we both functioned in the same way physically. We would smile and understand what creasing up the corners of our mouths meant. If we each produced a photograph of a man, we would be able to share an understanding that it represented someone important to us.

Human societies do have a number of very basic rules and laws in common. This is simply because humans are similar to each other in several important ways and when they live together they are bound to do certain things in the same way, whatever time and place they inhabit. Some writers have talked about the 'Golden Rule' and have attempted to show that it is the basic rule in all the major world religions and cultures. 'Do as you would be done by' is one way of putting it, or, 'Don't do to others what you would not like done to yourself.' Jesus said, 'Do to others what you would have them do to you, for this sums up the Law and the Prophets.' Such a rule certainly applies if you are about to hit someone on the head and steal their life savings. It is a universal rule that applies to everyone in the world. Even the thief does not want someone else to do this to him! He is not being a violent thief because he does not believe in this rule, or in more specific rules against stealing. He is just suspending the rules for a time!

There are a number of laws and rules that all humans and human societies have in common. These are universal laws, firstly because all humans have certain basic needs that have to be met, and secondly because unless we do certain things in a certain way human social life would not be possible. Lying works only because most of us tell the truth most of the time. Stealing would cease to be profitable if we all stole. All human societies, for example, have some form of marriage to regulate sexual relationships and the care and upbringing of children. The rules and customs about marriage, family and kinship are some of the most important.

The forms that marriage takes may vary—in some places, women have to marry their cousin on their father's side; in others, men are able to marry more than one woman. Some may divorce and re-marry; in other societies that may not be possible. Sex may be permitted before marriage, but usually there are strict laws or customary rules against adultery. In some places, children may inherit through their mother, and their uncle—their mother's brother—may be more important in their lives than their father.

But the basic structures which include very strong rules forbidding adultery and incest and setting out forms of inheritance are often very similar worldwide and throughout time. They are there because human children take many years to come to maturity and to learn all they need to know to take their place in adult society. These structures of family life hold a society in a pattern; they give boundaries that should not be crossed. There are, of course, always some who for a variety of reasons break the mould, or cross the forbidden boundaries; but what happens to them, if the consequences are severe, can reinforce the power of the rules. When the boundaries and the rules begin to change and become fuzzy and not so clear-cut, life can be exciting but also risky and threatening.

These very important areas of human life—marriage, parenting, kinship, owning land and houses, leaving them to your children when you die—are governed by a range of rules. Some of these are laws made by the state; some are the custom of the group and enforced simply by the pressure of the disapproval of neighbours and family.

In some societies, these rules are not easily broken: the punishments and the consequences may be so severe that no one would contemplate breaking them and staying within that community. This is sometimes the way things happen in traditional, small societies that have not been very much affected by the modern world. But at the other end of the scale, in the big cities of the developed and developing world, people may still think that rules about marriage, faithfulness and sexual restraint are important, but it is far less likely that they will be punished for not keeping them, and their neighbours may not even know what they are doing, let alone disapprove.

All societies have rules about land and property, and how it is owned, and there are usually laws about stealing. However, sometimes the laws only apply within the local group. You may keep your own group's laws about stealing, within the group, but it may be perfectly acceptable to steal from outsiders. Or one group's definition of stealing may be quite different from another's. There are tales of one Native American group who viewed all personal property as belonging to the whole group and expected anyone who had more than someone else to redistribute it. If a member of the group kept more than they needed, then they were stealing from the others. If they did not give away their surplus, then it was perfectly proper for someone else to do the redistributing for them. When white settlers arrived with more blankets, horses, ploughs, food and clothing than the Native Americans, then this particular group immediately stepped in and 'helped' them to distribute these items to the wider community. That is an extreme example of a very different understanding of what stealing means.

When asked about stealing and whether it is wrong, most people will grade different forms of stealing from very wrong to possibly not wrong at all. Stealing from your own mother might be at the top, and stealing from the taxman at the bottom. We can see that a rule which says 'Do not steal' may appear in some form in every human society, but it may be understood in very different ways.

Murder is another universal prohibition. But we have to be careful to understand exactly what we mean by murder. It hardly ever means that no one under any circumstances is to be killed. The state or the group decides what kind of killing is lawful, and when we talk of murder we mean unauthorized killing. In most societies, becoming a soldier and killing enemy soldiers in war is not forbidden, nor (in some countries) is the use of capital punishment by the state. Of course there are groups who believe that other killings are not wrong either. Urban guerrillas and terrorists will kill and bomb on the streets of a city that is not at war, but they will claim that they are soldiers fighting their own war and therefore justified in using guns and explosives. In the same way, these groups sometimes 'execute' opponents, claiming that their secret courts are legitimate and have the authority to order such punishment. In some societies, revenge killings—a killing for a killing—are against the law of the land but acceptable to the group that practises such a vendetta. On the other hand, there are those who do think that all killing is wrong, and that may bring them into conflict with their state if they are ordered to join the army and fight.

These and other rules and laws are common to all human societies. They may vary and come in different forms but they are recognizably similar, even though we do not normally learn them from some universal rulebook. There are universal moral declarations: some of the United Nations documents such as the Declaration of Human Rights would come into this category. Most of the rules and principles we live by, however, come to us within the groups to which we belong. Our schools, our parents and our society teach us right and wrong as we grow up, although increasingly each of these three may be giving us some rules that contradict each other.

One of the most important groups we belong to is our nation or state. We are expected to obey its laws, support its sports teams, pay taxes to run it, respect its institutions, honour its head of state, and fight in its wars. If we disagree with what its leaders do, we may be able to oppose them within the system, while still remaining loyal. That is one of the meanings of democracy. If we give away its secrets to an enemy, then that is called treason and usually carries the most severe penalty of the law.

Nationalism can be a most forceful source of ideas of right and wrong, and other rules can simply be swept away if it is the main guide to behaviour. We can see how that happens when we look at the history of Europe in the last century. In Bosnia, neighbours who had known each other for many years condoned the murder and brutalization of each other's women and children in the name of nationalism. In those circumstances, trying to keep any other rules needed courage of the highest order.

We have seen these kinds of tensions in other episodes of European history. Those who opposed Hitler in Nazi Germany were punished for treason and disloyalty, but some thought they should obey rules of a different kind because they loved Germany enough to oppose and defeat her government. Conscientious objection to serving in the armed forces of a country presents the same kind of dilemma, deciding between what nationalism requires, and what loyalty means. Not many of us are faced with that kind of dilemma, although we all need to work out just what our priorities are, in case we do one day have to make these tough decisions.

There are other groupings that determine what actions we think are right and wrong, and they too may come into conflict. Mary, in our last chapter, belonged to an ethnic minority in the United Kingdom. In every possible respect she is British—in language, in education, in the way she lives and works—but because to some people she looks Indian and not 'British' to them, their group loyalty works like a form of nationalism, and excludes her from their group. They might see her as a threat to their group's way of life and, because of that, will consider it right to be rude, to tell her to leave the country, and in some cases to threaten her and others like her with violence.

Belonging to a group can be a great source of comfort, support and comradeship. But it can also lead to an attitude which means that those outside the group are excluded and denied justice and consideration. It is a feeling that has helped armies to fight wars, colonialists to colonize and football club supporters to be enthusiastic, shout on the terraces and fight in the streets. This desire to exclude outsiders, however needy, also fuels the strong reaction some people have to those seeking asylum, having fled persecution or famine and disaster.

Although this sense of group solidarity can work in other less violent ways, these other ways can still deny the rights of others. The middle-class suburb which mobilizes to insist that a new road goes through another area of town, rather than their own, is working on group solidarity. The school class that will not tell the teacher who broke the window is being loyal to the group. Ideas of right and wrong, the rules you think you live by, can be sorely tested when group loyalty is at stake. Sometimes the police find that all witnesses to a terrible crime stay silent, because they will not break ranks with their group.

So the groups that we belong to can be very important in forming our own rules of good and bad, right and wrong, and sometimes they will differ from another group, in the same way that Robin Hood differed from the Sheriff of Nottingham over who should be taxed and where the money raised should go! We may be born in the same society, but these kinds of differences can lead to very different attitudes to right and wrong. The director of a multi-national company building a dam in a developing country may have a very strong sense that it is wrong to steal, and could say that he had never stolen anything in his life, even to the the extent of putting 50p in the box when he made a private phone call from the office. But those who are losing their land and their homes because of the dam may well think that what he is doing to them is a form of stealing.

When societies are very self-contained and members rarely meet anyone from outside their culture, they often assume that their way of doing things is the only right way. Seeing chopsticks used for the first time can seem not only odd but also bad table manners to knife and fork users. Talking to strangers on the London Underground can seem rude and pushy; not talking to strangers can seem rude and unfriendly. We have to learn to work out what rules are really about right and wrong, and which ones are simply taste and preference. We can see this very clearly when we look at dress codes. Strict dress codes are much less common than they used to be; wearing ties or hats is no longer obligatory in certain places. Women's dress worldwide, however, is still strongly influenced by ideas of modesty and decency. Islamic codes vary, but nearly all Islamic societies expect a far higher degree of covering-up than other countries. Most Westerners would probably use the word 'inappropriate' for a girl wearing a bikini in the high street, but a number of societies would see it as far more serious, even deeply immoral, behaviour.

All this means that most Westerners may believe that there are broad boundaries that people should not cross in their way of dressing, but we do not bother about it that much. We have become culturally tolerant, and understand that the definition of modest dressing varies round the world, and in different social groups. This development makes it easier for different groups to live together, often making allowances for each other—leaving the bikinis at home when on holiday in some parts of the world. But learning to be tolerant can sometimes mean that we learn to turn a blind eye to abuses of human rights that should not be tolerated anywhere.

When we are born, we join a human family, within a group, in a society that may be part of a larger nation state. We grow up learning from those around us all the different rules and principles, proverbs and guidelines which teach us how to live as members of those groups. We may be rebellious enough to want to challenge some of them. We may fight against our elders' way of seeing the world because we think it is out of date. And it is as children that we learn most of these ways of thinking about the world.

CHAPTER 4

The importance of parenting

How do we learn the rules? Most of us can remember our parents teaching us table manners. We can remember being told to share with our brothers and sisters, to be polite to aunts and uncles, to wash behind our ears and to get up in the morning. We may have been taught to stand up for the National Anthem, and to stand up when someone comes into the room.

Some of the basic ways in which we function as human beings, we learn as very small children. Studies in psychology have shown us that, for example, babies recognize the human face at a very early age, in a matter of weeks from birth, and moreover that they smile when they see one! They learn to respond with trust and confidence to human voices and human touch. We can understand why babies and young children who are denied loving human contact in their early months and years are unable to learn how to relate to other people and will, in most cases, grow up to be damaged adults. They may well have a very faulty idea of good and bad behaviour. They may have become used to riding rough-shod over others to get what they need and want. They may be unable to love properly and they may well be inadequate parents themselves, passing on their damage to the next generation.

These are extreme cases, yet at a much less serious level we may be influenced in ways we cannot help and may not even be aware of. Many babies born in the 1930s and 1940s were looked after by parents who had read babycare books which encouraged parents to be very rigid, to keep to strict timetables, to leave babies to cry until the right time for feeding and not to 'spoil' them. Babycare books have come and gone since then. Those written in the 1990s were far more likely to give parents permission to respond to their babies on demand, to cuddle them as much as they wanted, to tell them how wonderful they were and generally be as loving as possible. The interesting question is whether these two ends of the spectrum mean that these babies grow into adults who act morally in different ways. It would be too crude to expect the first group all to be very orderly, tidy, legalistic, driven people and the second group to be happy-go-lucky, loving and spontaneous, easily breaking the rules, but there just might be an element of truth in this.

One of the basic groupings of humankind is, of course, being male or female. Many of the groups we have mentioned in the last chapter include both men and women. Does our gender influence the rules we grow up with, and the way we make decisions about right and wrong?

One writer, an American Christian psychologist, has suggested that it does. What she says helps us to see how our ethical behaviour, why we obey rules and the way we obey rules, can be influenced by the way boys and girls are parented when very young. Somewhere around the age of three or so, small children get to know that they are a boy or a girl and that they will be that for ever. From that moment on, one of the things they need to learn is what it means to be male or female. Children learn this, and all the other things that they need to understand to be a social human being, from the adults round them—from the way they are handled, loved and disciplined; from what they see of adult relationships and behaviour. It is unconscious learning and happens, in the main, long before we have any formal education.

Small babies are mainly cared for by their mothers. In some rural traditional societies—and in our own in the past—this caring for young children was not so isolated but happened within a wider community of fathers and uncles, brothers, sisters and cousins, aunts and grandparents who were often part of the babies' daily lives. There were a number of role models to help the toddlers learn what being male and female meant in their society. But in many countries today, particularly in North America and Western Europe, mothers frequently bring up babies on their own. There are several reasons for this, such as the far greater number of lone parents these days, a very high proportion of those being mothers. In addition, work patterns frequently mean that the male breadwinner of the family works outside the home and some-times quite a long way away. He may also work very long hours and be away from home for most of his infant sons' and daughters' waking hours. Studies in the United States have shown that fathers spend very little time—sometimes less than ten minutes a week—in face-to-face communication with their babies. And even when fathers are at home, many groups do not consider the care of babies to be a role for men.

We have, then, a small boy or girl whose first and main love is their mother. Their passion is for her and all she provides. She has also been their role model, as she has taught them the whole range of skills including language, social habits and attitudes to others, through her encouragement, tones of voice, and so on. When the light dawns about being male or female, the child then needs a role model for this gender identity, and immediately a different learning path emerges for boys and for girls. The little boy has to learn that his mother is not his role model: there are some essential ways of being human, for him, that he cannot learn from his ever-present loving mother. His role model is, in a significant percentage of cases, absent, distant, and may not care for him in a way he understands. The girls have some advantage here because they can slip into female roles if they love their mother and want to copy her.

The studies seem to show that the upshot of this difference in learning how to be male or female is that the boys' rather uncomfortable learning process leads to a male tendency to be more determinedly male than the women are female. Their maleness may be aggressive and they will deny traits in themselves that they consider female. This can lead to the kind of male group behaviour that is belligerent and aggressively masculine. They may have a strong sense of what behaviour is 'manly' especially in relation to small children, and thus repeat the process with their own sons, finding it hard to be 'womanly' with their own small babies.

There is a difference, then, in how men are masculine and how women are feminine. They are not just mirror-image processes. The men assert their masculinity; the women simply accept that they are feminine. One possible outworking of this, though hard to measure, is that the girls tend to find it easier to start up and maintain relationships, they are more likely to be peace-makers, they will accept a fair amount of ill-treatment without seeking redress, and will count people as more important than principles—whereas men, in their work, and sometimes in their personal relationships as well, will see rules as more important than people.

Of course, like all trends and tendencies measured by social scientists, these effects of the under-fathering of young children only show when large numbers of people are studied. No one can say in an individual case that they are the way they are because of how they were brought up. The processes are too complicated and there are too many other factors at work to be precise about such things. But we can begin to understand that because, within a society, children are brought up in one particular way, certain tendencies in the way we decide about right and wrong are built into our communal life. It could be that the high crime rates for young men and boys, and the numbers of isolated, malfunctioning family groups of women alone with their children, are caused in part by the way babies are learning their gender roles. In the boardrooms of companies, the males may want to get on with the agenda and act with decision and sometimes with ruthlessness, and the females may want to consider the effects of decisions on employees and to spend more time talking. Although we should not exaggerate these differences, we need to acknowledge their existence and realize that they may be caused by certain styles of parenting.

At the beginning of the book, we eavesdropped on Peg and John and their decisions about their conservatory. It could be that Peg will want to accept the generosity of the builder, even if it is illegal, and John will want to tell him man-to-man that he has to obey the law. The difference between them could be the result of their parents' generation's belief that fathers should not be involved in the care of young babies. That may seem an exaggeration but it does point to the possibility that men and women have different ways of deciding right and wrong, because they have been brought up to think of male and female behaviour in certain ways.

Are you male or female, white or black, a lawyer or a bus driver, young or old, British or Indian? All of these groupings shape the rules that guide our moral thinking and make us more likely to decide to act in one way rather than another. Much of the groundwork of this shaping goes on in the first years of our lives. How were you brought up? Or rather, how was your generation brought up? Are you bringing up your children in the same way as your parents and grandparents did?

Sitting down to talk through issues of good and evil with a group of people from a variety of backgrounds, we can sometimes see how our group differences and upbringing have shaped us. On some topics, the women will have a bond that unites them against the men. On other topics, it will be the highly educated, or the young, or the rural dwellers who will feel that they share common causes and common beliefs. What unites us is the importance of the experiences that shaped us in those first few crucial years of our lives.

CHAPTER 5

Different sorts of people

We have looked at the kinds of rules that we acquire as we grow up as part of various groups. Our ethnic group, our nationality, our religious faith, our social class, whether we live in a large city or a small rural village, and whether we are male or female may all play a part in shaping the rules we share with the others in our group. As we grow older, our own age group may retain a number of rules that younger age groups have abandoned for newer ones. These rules and customs come to us in many different forms. Some groups may have unwritten rules about such things as the rudeness of staring, or pointing with finger or foot at another person. Most groups think that you should not be rude, but what is rude and what is not has to be learnt and can be very different in different places.

This process of learning both the big and the little rules, which is sometimes called 'socialization', happens through our family, our schooling, our friends, and all the media systems from books to television and the Internet. In the last chapter, we looked at one example which showed how the way in which toddlers are brought up may contribute to the differences between men and women in their attitudes to principles and relationships. We also differ, not just because we belong to different groups but because we all have different personalities.

Bill and Jean have a young son of three who has begun to behave in unacceptable ways at meal times. He will not eat what he is given, he wants to get down, he demands different food, screams and cries if forced to stay at the table. It is a phase with which many parents are familiar. Bill and Jean decide on a course of action. They know they need to handle their son in a consistent way, and both agree to say and do the same things. They begin on a programme of cuddling and making a fuss of him when he is amenable, and ignoring him when he begins to create a scene at the table.

Bill is tough, cool and simply goes ahead with the planned strategy, including any punishment. Jean feels the need to soften Bill's handling and to be far less direct herself. She will be conciliatory, often giving the child another chance, and another, and possibly another!

Bill wants Jean to act like him and cannot understand why she does not. It is totally clear to him that their decision is the right way forward and, anyway, they have decided and that is the end of it. If the programme does not work after a reasonable time, then they will have to think again. Jean is not sure and wants plenty of time to work out whether she does think this is right. Bill feels that they have made their plans and decisions and all they have to do is to act on them. Jean still feels that the plans are open for discussion, and is uncomfortable and stressed by the pressure Bill is putting on her.

Bill and Jean do not disagree about what is right or wrong. They simply work things out in different ways, but unless they can understand the differences between them and explain how they feel to each other, they are in for a very stormy time with growing misunderstandings.

Human beings differ in their personalities, their temperaments. These differences are not a characteristic of any particular group, but are distributed, as far as we know, through all groups, generations and societies. Personality and temperament characteristics are not right or wrong in themselves, though. They are simply different ways of being right and wrong, and Bill and Jean need to understand this. They need to see that Bill's strongly rational 'thinking' way of behaving clashes with Jean's very intuitive 'feeling' way. When they understand that, they may become a very powerful partnership.

As individuals we may be people-centred extroverts, or inner-world introverts; we may prefer conversation to silence or vice versa. We may have a strong sense of order and systems, or we may be very easy-going and accepting of others. Knowing the kind of person we are and knowing how others differ from us is an important part of making decisions, even big ones. We need to know where our weaknesses are and where we are too strong. We need to be able to work with others and live with others, and an understanding of human personality differences really helps.

There are a whole range of other factors that influence the way we decide about good and bad, right and wrong. Many of them come from the way we have grown up and what has happened to us. There are differences between first and subsequent children. Some parents are strong disciplinarians; others leave their children more or less to bring themselves up. Our school may have encouraged us to be very cooperative in the way we learnt and played games; another school might have encouraged a great deal of competitiveness. We may have been bullied. We may have been small for our age for many crucial years of adolescence. These kinds of factors can make us feel worthless with a very low sense of our own abilities, or very anxious to please, willing to do many things that we actually think are wrong in order to win praise and be accepted in a group.

Unemployment, ill health or depression should not change our beliefs about right and wrong, but they can. They can deeply change the way we see the world. If we become bitter and judgmental, or feel that the world owes us a living and that others have unfair advantages, then this can change the way we behave towards others.

All of these factors interact with each other. There are not many people who were brought up in such a way that they are totally well-balanced, with a good understanding of themselves and a sensible, caring system of ethics that is comprehensive and not contradictory. Nor are there many who go on to work well in their chosen job, have long-term happy relationships and are free from any real testing of their views of the way the world works. We all stumble along the way, and we stumble for different reasons and in different ways. Even where someone seems to have arrived at a balanced and good life in terms of their work and their family, they can still make disastrous decisions, break up their relationships, or leave their job for another, even though it is obvious to everyone round them that they are throwing everything good away.

CHAPTER 6

How will it all work out?

Jim is the managing director of a firm in the West Midlands, who is negotiating a contract with a government in South-East Asia. If he is successful, over one hundred jobs will be secure for several years. He has been asked for a fairly substantial sum by the agent who will arrange the contract with the government. Is this a bribe? If so, should he pay it? Should he consider the jobs in his home town and pay the bribe because he knows that that way he will make a fairly large number of people secure in their jobs and contribute to the well-being of the community?

We often make decisions based on the expected results of our actions as well as, or instead of, following the rules. There are situations when it is very important to work out the consequences. The instructions may tell us to light the blue touchpaper, but if the rocket is pointing straight at us, then knowing the outcome can also be important!

Allowing the consequences to determine what we do, rather than simply obeying the rules or not, is not easy. Often, we do not know what the consequences will be. Jim is thinking of the results for his home town, but those are not the only consequences. It may not even occur to him that there are consequences for the business life of the country which is signing the contract with him. Sometimes there may be no rules to guide us; or the consequences are all ones that we do not like and we are faced only with poor choices.

Adrian is a nurse trained to work in disaster situations. In the refugee camp where he is responsible for the infant feeding programme, the rains have delayed transport and there is a shortage of food for the babies. Adrian thinks the programme should target those with the best chance of healthy survival; his assistant thinks they should concentrate on the weaker babies; a young new volunteer feels passionately that they should give all babies the same amount of food, even though it will be inadequate for them all.

In one way, taking account of the consequences is important. We need to take responsibility for what we do. If someone else is jumping a red light, we do not simply drive into them because our light is green and we're obeying the rules. People who argue against always telling the truth often point out that sometimes the truth is better not told because of the damage it will do.

If the rules of the refugee camp said that all babies should be given the same amount, because that is fair and treats them all equally, then Adrian might decide that he had to obey that rule. It is possible that a large number of the babies would die. However, if his experience tells him that there is only enough food for 20 per cent of the babies, then he may calculate that that will be a better outcome than only a few surviving. He may judge that a percentage of the others will die anyway. In that way he will achieve the desired end—to keep as many as possible alive until the transport gets through with fresh supplies.

This kind of decision-making is sometimes called 'making the end justify the means'. In an extreme form we can use it to justify nearly anything. Governments with many people to please, and anxious to get re-elected, can often be guided in their decision-making by the outcomes of policies, rather than whether the policies are good or bad in themselves. The bombing of German cities and the dropping of the atom bomb on Japan, which took place at the end of World War II, have been justified by the argument that they brought the war to a more rapid conclusion and therefore saved many thousands of lives. Those in favour of these actions say that the 'means' were terrible, but the outcome meant that on that occasion the means were right. That does not mean that it will always be right to use such weapons. In fact, most people would say that in most cases it would be very wrong to use them. Nor was it possible at the end of World War II to see clearly what effect such actions would have on the relationships between the nations of the world in the future. There were more far-reaching consequences that very few could see at the time.

All rules have their exceptions, and sometimes the expected consequences can mean that a rule should be broken. This would be the justification for killing someone who had an automatic weapon trained on a large number of people. It might be the justification for stealing food to feed a starving family.

Some of the difficult ethical decisions taken in hospitals with limited resources, and unable to treat everyone, are made on the basis of achieving the greatest number of good outcomes. If a hospital only has room to treat one person for kidney failure, do they treat the professor who is doing cancer research but who also beats his children, or the tramp who is always kind? Should they value what someone has already done in their life, or give the young person a chance? How does a hospital decide between giving ten people new hip joints, or giving one person a new heart?

Making decisions based on the consequences is not an easy thing to do. Most of us do not know what is going to happen in the future and we do not know all the factors influencing the present. Our West Midlands managing director, Jim, may decide that paying the bribe is justified because so many people will keep their jobs at home. But he may discover a group of businesspeople in the country with whom he is making the contract who are desperate to end this kind of corruption. They have appealed to Western firms to support them and refuse bribes, so that the country's economy and reputation will improve, which will be better for them all. If he discovers this too late, he may find that he has seriously damaged a cause he basically approves of, and has lost the trust of some of his business partners in that land.

We should take into account the consequences of our actions because that is the responsible thing to do, but we need rules as well. We cannot sit down at each crossroads in our lives and work out from scratch all the ins and outs of every possible course of action. Jim knows that bribery is wrong. It is not fair. It means that the contract may go to the weaker firm or the more unscrupulous. The rule provides some stability in the situation. It warns him that he might be deceiving himself that he is doing the best for everyone, when he is simply doing the best for his own company and its employees.

Rules can also be very blunt and insensitive, however. Calling a payment a bribe might be unfair. It might be a legitimate form of commission. Looking at the context of the payment within the culture of the contract-signing country might show Jim that he should be paying it. Rules may be obeyed blindly without any thought being given to the principle behind them, rather like obeying instructions to 'shut the gate' into a field which has lost all its hedges.

Sometimes we know the rules we would like to follow, but we also need to take responsibility for what will happen as a result of our action. It is possible sometimes that rules have to be broken because the result—the end—does justify a different way forward. The difficulties come in trying to decide what exactly the consequences will be and whose benefit we are seeking.

CHAPTER 7

Doing what I feel like

'You don't know how it will feel,' Susan had argued when her evening class was talking about capital punishment. 'How can you know that capital punishment is wrong, until someone you love has been murdered?'

How important is the way we feel? When we have to make up our minds, should we listen to our feelings first and foremost; or should we do what the rules say, even if that goes against our feelings? Very few of us have to face terrible situations where someone has seriously harmed someone we love. But there are many situations where the way we feel can be a very powerful factor.

Joan disliked one of her colleagues at work and avoided her as far as she could. One day, as she parked her car in the company car park, she noticed that the colleague's car had been left with the headlights on. She didn't tell her. She pretended to herself that she hadn't noticed.

Emma was having a wonderful time with a crowd of friends at a local club. As the evening wore on, she was becoming more and more involved with Peter. She knew that if she did not go home before midnight, there would be big problems at home and she probably would not be able to come out again for some time. But alcohol and the excitement and strength of feeling he aroused in her were too much for her. She stayed with him all night.

Love, sex, revenge, malice, greed, and even joy and happiness, can all betray us when we are overwhelmed by them. Powerful emotions can lead us to act in ways that we then bitterly regret for many years afterwards. Many marriages and partnerships are broken because of the strength of overwhelming emotions at one particular moment for which many of us are ill prepared.

Why do most of us think that Joan was wrong not to tell her

colleague about her car? Would failing to tell her be right if the colleague was a very unpleasant person whom everyone disliked? Would it 'serve her right'? Do these emotions make any difference to the rights and wrongs of the situation?

Emma knew, even at the time, that she was going to regret what she was doing. She lived through consequences that meant she was not able to see Peter again and a relationship that she would have valued enormously was destroyed. Her relationship with her parents was also damaged.

But of course feelings and emotions do not always lead us to act in ways that we would normally think were wrong. They can also drive us to do what is right. Love can lead to heroism and endurance. Righteous anger can lead people to confront evil. When someone we love is hurt, we may look for the causes of that hurt and try to make sure that they cannot happen again.

Feelings can be a powerful driving force, but we need to know where we are being driven. The rules we live by and the consequences of what we do are important, and if they are drowned out by strong feeling, then terrible things can be done by normally good people. We can be seriously tempted to make exceptions for ourselves. We lose our temper and convince ourselves that it did us and the other person a lot of good by 'clearing the air'. We want to get our own back for some slight and convince ourselves that we are being just. We break a promise because we feel we should not have made it in the first place.

What protects us from being at the mercy of our feelings? The rules we have are not always clear-cut, as we have seen. They may conflict with each other, or we may not know which ones to apply. The consequences may not be clear and the choices might be difficult. We do not, however, come to each situation and work out how to act from first principles each time. We are already fully formed human beings. We already have a temperament and shaped individuality that will make it more likely that we will do one thing rather than another. The kind of person we are will be crucial in framing the directions our lives take, and the way we deal with our emotions. We need to know ourselves. We need to understand that we might be swept away by strong attraction, as Emma was, and prepare ourselves with that self-knowledge before the evening begins. We need to know that we react sharply and sometimes vindictively towards someone who irritates us, and prepare to control our tongue before we meet them.

If we are asked what kind of person we would like to be, I wonder how we would answer. What kinds of good points would we like to have? What are the virtues we value? When we know the answers, we are on the way to becoming the kind of person who can deal with decisions in a way that fits our ideas of what is best. We are less likely to be betrayed by the suddenness of events, and our own emotions, into going in the wrong direction.

When people are asked in polls what kind of characteristics they like best, they nearly all list traits like generosity, kindness, tolerance and gentleness. Joan in the car park knew it was wrong not to tell her colleague about the car and leave the battery to run down. If she had valued kindness and generosity in herself as well as in others, then she would perhaps have been governed by them rather than by her dislike. As a result, she might have ended the day with a sense of well-being instead of miserable guilt. Going to her colleague with a simple message about her car might have been the beginning of a new and better relationship in the workplace.

The importance of virtues that we value is that they are also feelings. They not only lead us to act in a certain way but they also help us to feel in a certain way long before we need to act. The big question is, what virtues should we develop and encourage in ourselves and in our children? The ones we listed—generosity, kindness and tolerance—are popular ones, although if people are asked to go into more detail, then we find that there are qualifications. Generosity may not extend beyond close friends and family. Kindness may be extended to animals, but not to all humans. Some virtues are not so popular. As a child, I was often told that 'patience is a virtue', but I was never sure myself. I could see that patience sometimes led people to tolerate bad things without doing anything about them.

We can face many strong emotions when we are involved with bringing up children. Looking on from the outside can be very hard for aunts, uncles, friends and grandparents. Although the love for a child can be the strongest and most powerful emotion some of us ever feel, it can still leave us puzzled and adrift as we try to work out the best way to teach and guide that child. We know that weariness and the desire for a quiet life, at least for a short time, lead most parents to give in, bribe, break promises and change the rules at some stage or another. Fortunately, children are resilient and adaptable. But for some, the sheer inability to cope with small children can produce, on top of love, other powerful emotions of rage, despair and helplessness that can lead to emotional and physical abuse.

We have looked at various aspects of human decision-making. All of us have to decide what is right and what is wrong; what is good and what is bad; what we value and what we think is the good life. We have looked at a number of brief moments in different people's lives. These are all real situations, although, of course, I have changed the names and altered the facts a little.

We have all been shaped by a variety of influences. These include the way we are brought up and the society in which we live. We have, as a result, a whole range of different kinds of rules to live by, many of which we may never have thought much about. We may live by them, but we may also live by working out consequences, or we may be driven by our personalities and our emotions.

Many of us are also copying other people. We may wish to be people of a certain type, and sometimes we meet someone who is the kind of person we would like to be. We can see in them all the personal attributes that we admire. The most important 'copying' happens when we are small and we watch how the adults round us live, particularly our parents. Later we can see that idols and heroes play an important role in shaping older children's styles of living. Strong 'in your face' girl power in a pop group may encourage a greater sense of self-worth in young girls and a more belligerent attitude to parents, teachers and, of course, boys. In the world of popular culture, style can seem just a matter of dress and physical actions on stage, but such style can send powerful messages about attitudes to life. 'Doing it my way', 'All I need is love', and 'I want you now' are not usually the sentiments of trad-itional moral values!

Above all, we must remember that we do not stand alone. We live interrelated with other human beings. Round us the world is changing and new ideas are becoming popular; old habits and customs are disappearing and we face new challenges to our rules and our lists of virtues.

CHAPTER 8

Living in a changing world

There are a great many changes going on in the world today. Anyone who is much over 30 has seen a significant number already. Most of us are regularly brought up short by something that seems strange and new. Sometimes as I travel on the London Underground to work, I am aware that people are talking all around me, but no one is talking in English. That is partly due to the fact the most of the English are travelling to work silently, and all the others are tourists and holidaymakers in groups. But it does give me the odd feeling that I have dozed off and woken up somewhere else! We may get the same feeling listening to a crowd of young people talking in a pub, or switching between television channels late in the evening or surfing the Internet. Most of us sometimes wonder which planet we are on, when assailed by an information barrage from the new technology.

If the world changes, then the situations in which we have to decide what to do change. Of course, in one sense the world is always changing, particularly for individuals. We all grow up and grow old, and those basic 'unchanging' facts lead to changes in the way we live. The problems of adolescence are not the same as the problems of retirement. There have always been changes going on in society. People move from the village to the city. Populations grow and cause overcrowding. The economy falters and many people have no work. Wars are lost and won. Tragedy strikes a family or a whole community and all existing patterns of behaviour are called into question. Problems of good and evil become acute.

In the past, it may have been possible for grandparents to pass on to their grandchildren a full file of 'how to live' instructions, assuming that they would grow up, have a family and in the process meet no new situations nor have to adapt to new worlds that would make their grandparental instructions out of date.

But sometimes change can happen so fast and in so many different aspects of life that we encounter problems above and beyond the usual ones of adapting to old age and perhaps a little bit of economic inflation. Many writers think we are living in an age of that kind of change now, at the beginning of the 21st century, and they date the beginnings of the acceleration of change to the decades after World War II.

Mike, a fifteen-year-old boy, wrote to a national newspaper's dilemmas column with a problem. He and his mother lived together in a small flat. He was going on holiday to Greece with his mother and a woman friend of hers, and he had discovered that his mother and her friend intended to sunbathe topless. He was embarrassed and horrified, but his mother's response was to laugh at him, tell him not to be a prude, and remind him how much he would enjoy seeing the girls of his age topless.

A number of readers responded by being very sharp with Mike's mother for putting a fifteen-year-old in that position. Apart from the ethical issues that come out of the incident, however, we can also see evidence of many of the changes of the past fifty years. Greek society has adapted to the tourist trade in ways that would not have been part of their traditional Orthodox culture in the past! Mike lives with his mother without his father. Fatherless families and very small household units are features of the changes over the past thirty or so years. Mike's mother already behaves as if Mike were a friend or flatmate rather than a son, and as he becomes an adult she may prefer him to be just a companion and not a son who will leave her as soon as he is old enough to live away. Young men who live in the parental home well into adult life are another feature of today's world; the reasons may be partly financial, and partly the care and home comforts they are used to.

So let us look a little more closely at particular areas of change and see how they make a difference to our efforts to do the right thing in the dilemmas that face us.

Some of the most dramatic changes have happened in family life and relationships. Most of us are familiar with these: an increased divorce rate, so that around half of marriages break up; an increasing number of people who are not legally married but live together in partnerships of varying length and commitment. These partnerships appear to last for a shorter time and break up more easily than those between people who have married legally. There are, therefore, far more people today who have had a number of partners in their lifetime. People are choosing to leave a partner and live with another, and they expect to be able to make that choice when they feel like it. That leaves a very different general social attitude to marriage from one where the end of a marriage usually comes through the death of a spouse.

Dramatic changes are also happening in parenting. More women are actually choosing not to have children even when they are married, and those who do have children are having them much later. Over a third of all children born are born to unmarried parents. Due to these changes, an increasing number of children live with only one parent, usually their mother. Others live in reconstructed families where there are half- and step-siblings, living with step-parents. These changes in family structures, which mean that more and more children do not complete their growing up with the same two male and female carers, are having a measurable effect on the health and well-being of those children. Divorce and separation are among the main causes of poverty, and poverty has adverse effects on children. But some evidence is now indicating that poverty is not in itself the main cause of emotional distress and poor school performance in children. It is the loss of a parent that is the main problem, even if that parent keeps up some contact.

We have a growing number of more complicated relationships, bringing additional strains on individuals who have to choose between competing bonds of love and commitment. Who looks after elderly grandparents, or visits a lonely aunt, when the family has split and reconstituted itself?

We have a growing number of smaller households. Many people live on their own. A large number of these solo households are the widowed elderly, mostly women, but increasing numbers of young unmarrieds, particularly young men, live alone. Many of these people have little contact with their families on a regular basis. If they have a social life it is usually with their own age group, so that they have little contact with people of a different age bracket from their own.

In these situations, the long-term promises and commitments of marriage, as well as the commitments that we are born with—to parents and sometimes to a wider kin group of aunts, uncles and cousins—are beginning to fade and become far more provisional. We can choose whom we relate to, and at what depth and for how long. We may live alone for lengthy periods, with only transient relationships, perhaps intense, but frequently short-lived. In these situations, many of the rules and principles we have acquired about family life are difficult to apply. We make up our own according to popular trends and our own feelings and preferences.

We may be able to replace a lover or a friend and move on with few regrets, but to remove a parent from a child who has no choice is devastating for them. When we simply offer them a replacement we may in fact be breaking their hearts. In divorce, the loss is not restricted to a parent. Children also lose grandparents, cousins and other kin in the process of parental separation.

Jill moved in with Bob and his children when she was twenty. One day at work someone asked her how she related to the children and whether she found it easy to discipline them. 'That's nothing to do with me,' she replied. 'They aren't mine. They are around, but I don't take any notice of them.'

Here were three children under eight years old whose mother had gone, and who had an adult in the house who slept in their father's bed but made no attempt to relate to them in any way that would make sense to them.

We also live with enormous developments in technology. Some of these changes create new situations where, sometimes, we are not sure how to apply the moral principles we have grown up with. One of the areas most often featured in the national media is that of medical ethics. New technologies that increase the possibility of keeping people alive and deal with a range of diseases have caused new ethical problems. In the area of parenting, attitudes change because technologies change. Fifty years ago, couples who did not conceive had to accept their infertility, however devastating and disappointing they found it. Couples who found their fertility hard to control had to adapt to having more children than they would really have liked. Now that it is possible to control fertility, and to use medical technology to make conception happen, there is a growing sense that we have a right to have children, or not to have children, when we wish. In this area we no longer accept what life brings and accept the obligations to care and nurture. All the possibilities of *in vitro* fertilization, the use of donor sperm and eggs, surrogate motherhood, and even freezing sperm so that widows can have their dead husband's children, raise difficult ethical issues.

Many of these issues are new, while some have to be worked out by the health professionals involved—for example, whether an unmarried woman of sixty should be treated so that she becomes pregnant. But they also have to be worked out by the whole of society so that the right laws can be passed. This means that all of us individually need to be aware of these issues and be able to think through what laws we would like to see in place. There are many old rules that come in to play—rules about parenting by mothers and fathers, about whether we do have a right to have children; whether children should be conceived for our pleasure; whether the 'natural' way of sex and conception is the right way and all artificial ways are wrong.

From the beginning of life, with decisions about using the new technology to keep alive tiny premature babies, to the end of life and the issues involved in the use of life support systems, health professionals are faced with difficult ethical decisions. And the doctors and others involved do not want to have to make these decisions on their own. They want all of us to help, and when we are patients or relatives of patients, we too can be presented with difficult decisions.

Technology and scientific understanding of ourselves and our world, as well as a greater access to information through television news, have brought other new moral questions to tax us. Here are some questions that no one even thought about until sometime in the last thirty years.

If it is right to look after my health and that of my household, should I buy genetically engineered tomatoes? Should I consider the cholesterol in the food I buy? Should I feel guilty about smoking? Should I stop my children sunbathing?

If all they say about the environment is right, should I recycle my glass and newspapers? Should I use disposable nappies for my babies? Should I drive the children to school when it is only a mile away? Should I buy a mahogany loo seat? Should I have a second car?

There are other areas of awareness that have also brought new moral issues into our lives. We are presented with a greater array of information about our world and all its diversity and its tragedies. When we are presented with appeals for help for disasters in distant corners of the world, we see people give generously to famine, drought and earthquake victims. But doesn't charity begin at home? Do these people overseas deserve to be helped? If they have been involved in civil war, then aren't they just getting what they deserve? Should we give to countries where corrupt governments and officials will siphon off all our aid for themselves? We end up involved in ethical discussions that require a great deal of information to work out the right or wrong response.

Another area where new ethical obligations have been laid on us is in the care and management of animals. Should we campaign to ensure that animal species do not become extinct? Should we eat meat? Should unwanted pets be put down, even though they are healthy? Should animals be trained to perform in circuses? Should farm animals be raised intensively? Should we only buy free-range meat and dairy products? Should governments compel the fishing industry to stop fishing until stocks are replenished? Should permission be given to develop a site that has rare birds and butterflies living on it?

The world is changing. Do we have to change with it? Is it going off in the wrong directions? Should ideas about right and wrong also change or should they be the same whoever and wherever we are? Should we be resisting all the modern trends? If so, what exactly are the underlying attitudes that are part of our new world?

CHAPTER 9

Underlying attitudes

For many of us, the closest we get to the world of exciting change and choice is through the media. Already we are seeing the beginnings of the explosion of channels that satellite and cable are bringing to our television screens, and the whole world of global information and entertainment is opening up through the Internet. It may seem an exaggeration to say that the whole world is changing at an increasing pace around us. Our lives at home and work, in small towns and cities, may not seem very different from those of our parents, but if you watch a variety of programmes from a number of channels for one evening you will not need to think very hard to realize that change is in the air.

Many of the underlying attitudes and assumptions about human behaviour have changed radically, yet there are also deep stabilities. When attitudes are measured and analysed over time, both the enduring continuities and the areas of change can be seen. Much of what we hear and see, particularly in the media, can seem so much froth and bubble, but underneath there are some very deep-down changes in what we value and what we wish for. We need to understand what some of these deep-down changes are.

We are expected to want more from life; we have more choice. Even at very ordinary levels, if we can afford it we can choose, from vast arrays, what food we eat, how we eat it and where. We can choose the image we want to put across in the clothes we wear. We can choose a myriad different places in which to take holidays. We are encouraged to choose schools for our children. We can choose to set up home in a range of different styles. We can entertain ourselves at home in a range of ways. Some of the greatest changes of recent years have come because we have so much choice. We can buy what we like, even if we do not have the ready cash, because so much credit is available. A couple of generations ago, many people had strong views about spending money, about waste, about the value of saving and about the irresponsibility of getting into debt. All that has changed.

We tend to see self-fulfilment as a very important aim in life. We value satisfaction and happiness. We often gauge the value of the things we do by the extent to which they satisfy us and fulfil us. Therefore, when we are bored with something, we do not easily endure it but will look for a way out. This low boredom threshold affects us particularly in the areas of life that do tend to be a little boring and do require some effort, like learning in school, and staying married.

The underlying belief that we owe it to ourselves to get the most out of life works in different ways for us. Of course it is not a completely bad thing. It can make us take opportunities and risks that enhance both our own and others' lives. But it can also make us far less willing to carry some of the burdens of life. It can lead to deep resentment if we have to look after disabled relatives, for example. It can give us an adequate reason to avoid some tasks that we simply don't like.

Derek developed a passion for languages as a young student. He combined that with his Christian faith and spent fifteen years in Papua New Guinea, happily and with great fulfilment, translating the Bible and other texts into several previously unwritten languages. When he was forty, his father died and his mother developed arthritis. He came home and looked after her in her small house in Indiana for the following fifteen years. He did some translation work during that time, but as it happened before the coming of computers, e-mail and fax, his contacts with Papua New Guinea were too intermittent for him to help his colleagues very much. He did his duty. He cared for his mother.

Many people who knew Derek thought that this was a terrible waste. What kind of popular appeal does that kind of devotion to duty have today? Most of us are already thinking of alternatives for Derek as we read this. Such a decision is difficult for many to comprehend: it meant not only the loss of his own self-fulfilment, but also the loss of work that would help many others, all for one old lady. We know too little about the details of this story to be able to say that he had no alternative, but not many would even contemplate such an act today.

We also value excitement and entertainment. For younger people, the fear of boredom or of missing the centre of the action can lead to a search for 'kicks', a willingness to do a lot to find new ways of being excited. If we have enough money, we will give our children computers and televisions in their bedrooms, and as a consequence make ourselves yet more isolated even in our homes. We will want the excitement of new food and drink, Thai cooking this year, Mexican the next; a party every weekend, so that festivals and birthdays are difficult to celebrate with feasts and presents, because we have banquets all the time and have already bought all that we could want.

.We value freedom as well as choice, and so we feel that obligation and duty are somehow restricting the freedom to which we have a right. It may be this that lies behind the significant drop in the number of couples having children. New parents feel the stress of the demands of babies, not just in the normal wear and tear of looking after small children, but in the affront that such obligations as getting up several times in the night present to their expectations of the good life and the free life.

We do not easily accept authority. We value freedom to choose when and whom we shall obey. No one can simply claim the moral authority to tell us what to do—not the police, not schoolteachers, not parents. When we are ordered to do something, we will want to know why, and will then decide whether we will do it or not.

We value tolerance. We do not like judgmentalism. Because we tend to confuse being judgmental with making judgments, then we stop making judgments. We begin to think that if people want to do things their way, who are we to suggest they are wrong? But of course, none of us is consistent. So some may argue passionately for freedom of the press and for no censorship, but also campaign for the banning of all handguns. The same ethical arguments about civil liberty and human rights arise in both, but we can reverse the arguments in each case. We may disapprove of capital punishment so strongly that we are willing to take up cases in other lands, but we may also be passionate advocates of freely available abortion, again reversing our use of arguments based on human rights and murder.

We all have some boundaries to our belief in tolerance. Everyone has something they think is wrong, whoever does it. Child abuse is in some ways the crime of the late 20th and early 21st centuries because we are now conscious of it and we have begun to find out that it has been going on undetected for years. More subtle forms of abuse, such as the pressure on the young to be sexually active at an early age, are accepted by many as only natural. When a child is sexually abused, and perhaps murdered, by a practising paedophile, there is an enormous outburst of anger, and media coverage has encouraged the searching out and hunting down of known paedophiles. But very few children are in fact abused and killed by strangers; most children are abused by their brothers, step-brothers and fathers. The mobs shouting outside the home of someone who they think is a paedophile are more than likely to include a number of family men who abuse the children in their care.

These changes are part of everyone's world. Of course, not everyone thinks the same way. However, with global markets and global communication systems, it is far easier for trends, ways of thinking, to become widely accepted very quickly compared with the past. The influence of the dominant media images, the soaps on television, popular newspapers and magazines is widespread.

There are some underlying trends that go in different directions. One of the stronger pressures is the importance of equality for different groups, as part of the human rights movement. There are strong pressures from some groups for black rights and the end of racism, for women's rights and the end of sexism, for gay rights and the end of discrimination on the basis of sexual orientation, for the rights of disabled people. At the same time in some parts of society, there is still a popular suspicion of such pressure, and a strongly white, male, or homophobic reaction can emerge. These tensions can erupt in a particular neighbourhood. Then ordinary people have to decide the rights and wrongs of these different attitudes, and take sides.

We can now add to sexism and racism a new discriminatory 'wrong'—that of 'speciesism'. Strong animal rights movements and some new philosophical thinking have questioned whether humans should continue to think of themselves as being special and different as a species. Humans are only another kind of animal but with more brain potential. When we argue for the right of humans not to suffer, we should argue instead for the rights of all animals that are self-aware and can feel pain. From this perspective, some of the higher apes have more rights than a newborn human infant or a senile elderly human. This view is not widespread, although the animal rights movement and the desire to see justice for animals is strong. But seeing humans as simply part of the wider physical environment, and nothing more, can lead to changes in attitudes to humans who are not useful, who cannot contribute to society, or who are in pain.

Change is exhilarating and exciting, especially for young people. As they experiment with new relationships, new forbidden substances, and new technologies, the roles and rules that their parents brought them up to live by often look increasingly out of date. And being out of date is not popular.

A changing world with changing patterns of family life, changing patterns of work and leisure, changing passions and obsessions, does make many of us feel insecure. It calls into question many of the rules and moral guidelines that we thought would never change and were basic to being human. We cannot go back to the old simplicities, where we did things in certain ways and had no need to ask any questions. Now we will have to think through everything we value. We will have to work out why we believe certain things are right or wrong. Otherwise we will find that we shall sink beneath the challenges that a new generation brings. There is no longer any such thing as the wisdom of the old. A technologically sophisticated world deskills the elderly, who cannot pass on knowledge acquired over a lifetime that simply no longer applies. In only a few places in the world are the 'elders' still honoured and considered 'wise'.

What can we do to maintain ourselves as people who know what they want to be like, who know what kind of good life they want to live, and who can make the right decisions at the right time?

We are aware that our personality and temperament lead us to react in different ways, that we have different values from other groups in society. How can we know which way is right? Is it possible to know? Or have we moved into a time when we can freely choose whichever rule we want to apply? Are we on our own? What happens to our lives in our communities if everyone chooses differently?

What will happen if we tell our children they can do what they like? Eat when they like and what they like? Have sex when they like and in any way they like? Work or not work? How can we train them to act in the ways that we think are right if everyone round us is doing something different? And will they listen to us anyway?

CHAPTER 10

What is ethics? What is morality?

Ethics is the name given to the study of morality. It covers ideas about right and wrong, good and evil. It looks at how humans make decisions about such things. It asks questions and tries to answer them, about what humans value, what they name as virtues and vices and how they come to decide what their duty is.

Ethics has usually been studied as a branch of philosophy as well as theology. Philosophy, the 'love of wisdom', involves asking all the deep questions of life—why we are here, who we are, why we live the way we do, whether the universe has a purpose. Philosophy is a way of thinking, a skill in working out ideas, in thinking logically and rationally. It is about understanding. It is not so much the study of *what* happens as of *why* things happen. It asks questions about ultimate meaning—whether there is a god, what he (or she) is like and whether we can know this god in any way that is worthwhile. Theology, the study of God, moves on to work out what we can know of God, how he communicates with us and what our response should be.

The two most fundamental questions of all are looked at by philosophers and theologians, although, in very different ways, they are also the basis of all other areas of learning, including science. They are so basic that if we could answer them completely we would be gods ourselves. If we could move outside time and space and look in on the universe, then we might know the complete answer. Yet these two questions need to be understood in some way or another before we can look at everyday ethics of ordinary people.

The first is how we can *know*. The second is how we can know that what we know is *true*. These may sound very theoretical, but they are important questions for morality.

If I say to a young person on a station platform, 'You should not knock that old lady down and take her handbag', he could reply, 'Why shouldn't I? I can do what I like. Who says it's wrong? Why should I listen to you?' If I reply, 'It says do not steal, and you should respect the elderly', he could reply, 'How do you know it says that? Where does it say it? Who says it? How do you know that those things are true? I believe you should look after yourself in any way you can and it doesn't matter about anyone else.'

The young man has a view of the world that is different from mine. But if I want to convince him that mine is better, I will have to explain how I know what I know and why I think what I know is true. Of course, we could be so cross with each other and so unused to logical thinking that a calm, intelligent philosophical discussion is unlikely to happen.

Moving on from knowledge and truth, we then have to ask the question, 'Who says that we *ought* to do something?' Where does the idea of obligation come from? The answers that philosophers have given to this question have fallen into several groups.

First, there are those who say that our ethics come from God. He has directly revealed to us what is right and what is wrong. In the Old Testament story of the Ten Commandments, God writes his laws on stone tablets, so that all the people of Israel know what is right and what is wrong.

Second, other philosophers have recognized that God is there, but they say that we know right and wrong because humans can work it out for themselves. We can 'read' the world and nature and see what is right and wrong, what is good and evil, because God has put it there when he created it all, but we don't need him to tell us directly.

Third, and coming later historically, others have emphasized that humans can work out their morals for themselves because we have our own rationality. We can think for ourselves. If God exists, he does not exist in the same way as the world of nature does. We cannot sense him in any way that has meaning. In the Middle Ages, philosophers thought that they could prove the existence of God by logical rational argument, but since then many would argue that we cannot know God with human sense or intellect. And if that is the case, then they would say that there probably is no God, at least not one that is of any consequence for human living.

Fourth, others say that there is no outside source, no God who created the world. Nor are humans able to think everything through and work everything out for themselves. They are not totally free, rational and logical beings. These days, philosophers are listening to those who study sociology, which says that humans develop and learn in society, and that the way humans think about the world is not a consequence of sitting down and thinking it all out. Even our ways of thinking are shaped and patterned by the way we have been brought up in a particular society.

Philosophers are also listening to psychologists, who describe the ways in which humans are shaped by unconscious forces, learning guilt and obligation not by thinking rationally, but by the way they are motivated by sex, or love, or power, or some other inner drive beyond their control. There are also biologists who study the whole animal world and link the understanding of good and bad to the basic instincts that we all share as earthbound creatures. Instincts, such as those of the territorial hunter, for example, lead to certain kinds of behaviour in humans just as in other species.

Of course there are many psychologists and sociologists, as well as philosophers, who also believe in God. Even they are now used to thinking about the way humans behave as if God does not exist, however, or at least as if he has nothing to do with what goes on.

The first important group of philosophers who wrote about ethics were the Greeks who lived 500 years or so before Jesus Christ. Among them, Plato, Socrates and Aristotle have had the most profound and long-lasting effect on the way we think. The Greek thinkers of that time have not only influenced philosophy, but every branch of human knowledge for the 2500 years since they were alive. Much of what they wrote became the cornerstone of Christian thought for many centuries, although they were not Christians.

The Greeks believed in a life after death. This has a very important effect on how we think about goodness, and the questions we ask about how an individual should live in order to achieve happiness. If we think we can only be happy in this world, we are unlikely to risk our lives to be good. If we believe in a soul that survives after death, however, and that we will be rewarded after death for being good, then we will be good even if we sacrifice our lives in the process. Socrates himself died because he would not change his mind about what was good.

Aristotle wrote about the need for humans to cultivate virtues—that is, a good character. In his list he included such things as courage and temperance, wisdom and understanding. This idea of virtuous character building is a very important one and has sometimes been neglected by those writing about ethics. They have tried to work out why we have rules of right and wrong, but have not asked what kind of people are likely to obey or disobey the rules. Aristotle's virtue of courage would obviously influence the way a person acted. Someone might be well aware that he should dive into a lake to save a child, but his level of courage, or cowardice, would be the important factor determining whether he did it nor not.

The Greek philosophers were aristocratic men who were the élite of their society, and so did not write about ordinary people. They thought that only philosophers, the ones who had the most wisdom and understanding, would be able to work out the best way to live. All the others —slaves, poor people and women—were of little consequence.

However, their ways of thinking about heaven, body and soul, good and evil had, in some ways, more influence on Christian thinking than did the original Hebrew ways of thinking that are found in the Bible. The great thinkers of the Christian Catholic Middle Ages, such as Thomas Aquinas, based their thought on the writings of the Greeks. Although deeply religious and never questioning the Christian faith they held, they believed that law, ethics and morality were there to be discovered for ourselves, 'written' in nature. Aquinas, for example, thought that the feudal order of kings, lords and serfs was 'natural'. He would have thought that a system that allowed all men, let alone women, to be equal was unnatural and therefore 'immoral'. The idea that there is a single moral law, based on what is 'natural', has been a strong element in Christian and particularly Catholic thinking.

This has influenced thinking in one very important area of life. The 'natural' purpose of sex, for example, is to have children, so that the human race continues. Accordingly, sex that does not have that purpose is unnatural and therefore immoral. It does not matter if conception does not take place, as long as it might have done, and so only sexual activity between a husband and wife using no artificial means of contraception is right. This is the kind of ethical argument, put rather crudely, that evolved from a 'natural law' view of human morality.

Before the 17th century, there was a widespread confidence in the existence of God. People also believed that values of right and wrong were absolute—that they did not change from place to place and from time to time. These values were also universal—right for everyone and applying to everyone. From the 18th century onwards, many philosophers and theologians lost this confidence. The radical changes of the industrial and political revolutions brought radical changes to thinking. It might be wrong to make small children work in factories from the perspective of one way of thinking, but factory production would in the end produce a great deal of happiness for large numbers of people. Therefore, others argued, it was better to work out the consequences for those large numbers and allow the means to justify the ends. New ways of living produced new ways of being moral.

All of us without exception are shaped and influenced by our times. Our history, our society, the ideas that are current at a given time, all go to make us the people we are. This is as true for all the thinkers, philosophers and theologians of the ages as it is for ordinary people. Sometimes we can look back and wonder how on earth past thinkers could not see something that is obvious to us. After we have learnt something, we forget what it was like not to know it! We can trace the influence of powerful new areas of thought—the new thinking of psychology and the writing of Sigmund Freud, for example—on the theologians of the early 20th century. At the same time, great thinkers push back the boundaries of ideas and do have new insights that escape from these shaping influences, but they can never be completely free from their time and place. This is a very important factor to bear in mind for ourselves, when we are reading or listening to the words of others.

More recently, philosophy has split into a number of different branches. Some have written about the meaning of words, arguing that we make words mean what we like. Words like 'good' and 'bad' simply are a way of saying that we like or do not like something, rather as if 'good' meant 'hurrah' and 'bad' meant 'boo'. 'Good' and 'bad' have no moral force; they are simply expressing personal preference, and to say that something is 'good' is meaningless. As a result, our ethics—our morality—is criticized and dismantled, but no one knows how to construct a new system for us all. We are left in a world that cannot discuss issues of good and evil, because we no longer know what each of us means. In a way we have simply cut off the branch on which we were all sitting. There is a sense in which the philosopher who is mugged on his way home from the university has only himself to blame. The trickle-down of his opinions has made it possible for a new generation to question all previous ideas of right and wrong.

How does a human being know what is right? How can we find agreement? Are we free to make up our own minds? If we do, what if our neighbours believe the opposite? We may be free to make moral choices, but are there moral choices to be made? I am an adult human being surrounded by others, some of whom I love and care for. I have some idea of what a good life means. I want to look back on my life and know that the things I did made the world a better place, that the people I knew and loved were glad that I was around. We are still where we were in the first chapter. We may understand a little more of what is involved, but many of us long for firmer ground.

CHAPTER 11

Looking at real problems

The last few chapters have looked at the theory and practice behind ethical decision-making. Now is the time to get back to real situations that we all have to face at one stage or another. We began the book with John and Peg in their conservatory. Let us look at some of the issues involved in their dilemma.

First, they have to decide whether or not to obey the law of the land. Most of us know that we should obey the law, but we do rank laws according to their importance, and we allow ourselves to decide whether there are circumstances in which we would disobey. The fear of being found out is a strong factor in obeying a law. Sometimes people think that a law is silly or wrong. If sufficient numbers simply disobey or ignore that law, then, depending on the kind of government, either the law will be scrapped, or people will be punished. I am sure that John and Peg would like people to pay their taxes; if no one paid them, the whole of our society would grind to a halt, not least the schools and the hospitals. Does their breaking the law in such a small way make the disintegration of society a little more likely?

Would it be possible for John and Peg to compromise? Could they say to the builder that they would wish to pay their own tax but it was entirely up to him whether he paid his tax or not? They may feel that he should pay his tax, but it is not easy for adults to tell other adults what they should or should not do. We do not admire people who are bossy and interfering.

John and Peg find it difficult to accept their daughter's complaint, not because she is wrong, but because she is their daughter. It is hard to be corrected by those we think should be listening to us. But if they can bring themselves to acknowledge her point and talk about ways to balance the money they are spending on themselves with some giving to others, then they might be beginning a new relationship with her.

In our second chapter, we met Mary, the doctor, and her husband Stephan. Their problems were more long-term than John and Peg's. They want to have children and bring them up in all the ways that they think are right. At the same time they want to keep working and stay in their chosen careers. These issues are not the same as a straightforward decision to break the law. However, Mary has been brought up in a culture which has strong views on the place of women. Her mother was certain that she should make a home for her children and her husband and should not go out to work. She saw her husband as the head of the household and the breadwinner. But Mary's parents also felt strongly that both their sons and their daughters should be given every opportunity to benefit from education. When Mary showed that she was academically able and won a place at medical school, they were proud and pleased. They were giving two different kinds of messages to Mary, not by what they said but more by what they did. How else could Mary show that she was indebted to them for the sacrifices they made to enable her to go through medical school than to work as a doctor, giving back to the community?

Stephan and Mary carry the guilt of not being sure whether they have made the right decision. They worry about the kind of care their children have been getting at nursery and with childminders. They have to plan for when the children are sick. They have to rely on neighbours and relatives to be back-up for them. When one of their children shows signs of rebellion or exhibits difficult behaviour, Mary and Stephan are forced to ask whether it is because of their own absence at work, or whether the children would have been like that anyway. It is just possible that they may discover one day that they were wrong to run their lives in that way—not necessarily because such a family pattern is wrong for everyone, but because it was wrong for them.

Here we have two couples trying to decide how to live. All round us, such choices are having to be made. It is not that facing problems is a new thing at the beginning of the 21st century, and that in the old days life was just plain sailing. But two changes have made our decision-making more difficult. First, all the new ways of thinking and living that we have outlined in the previous chapters have made us far less sure that we know the right route to take. Second, we have far more opportunities and choices. They make our lives more interesting but more complicated. If John and Peg had lived fifty years ago, they would probably not have lived in their own house, nor had enough money in late middle-age to build a conservatory; an extra room in which to catch the sun and grow plants would not have been an option. Most people paid each other in cash and there was no sales tax.

Had Mary been born fifty years ago in her parents' home town in India, she would have had some schooling, perhaps to the age of twelve or thirteen, and then she would have learnt domestic skills from her mother, and been trained to look after her father and her brothers. She would have been married at a young age by arrangement, and have slipped into the running of her own household.

Let us look at some other situations and examine what is involved in coming to an answer.

The Webbs are members of a small church in a pretty village. There are plans to build a new road across farmland very close to the village and church. The alternative route for the road is close to a fairly large housing estate on the edge of a nearby town and will require several houses to be demolished. A group of village activists, set up to oppose the route, come to the church's council and ask for their support, encouragement and active participation. At a very difficult meeting, the Webbs and their fellow church members try to decide how they should respond and on what grounds.

All round the world, communities face the pressure that growing populations bring. The need for roads, houses, land to grow food, and supermarkets with car parks, means that the environment is often threatened. Maybe an Indian village needs more land to grow crops, but the villagers want to use part of a National Park where several species of bird and mammal are threatened with extinction. The Webbs do not want to see their picturesque village spoilt; but are they justified, perhaps by self-interest, to campaign for the road to pass near someone else's house? They may feel that they should look at all the pros and cons and make an independent, objective judgment about which route is the best. But they have to live with their neighbours, some of whom are quite sure that they should fight to preserve their homes from such an intrusion, whatever it means for someone else.

Jenny has power of attorney for her elderly and very confused uncle. He is in a nursing home. Her nephew, from a different side of the family, has a desperate need for £8000, otherwise he will lose his small landscape business and his family home. Jenny could easily sign a cheque on her uncle's account, trusting that her nephew will be able to pay it back before it is needed. How should she decide what to do?

Jenny's problem is similar in one way to that of the Webbs above, and John and Peg and their builder. We know that it is probably right to go a certain way, but doing the right thing involves upsetting or disagreeing with someone else, sometimes someone whose opinion we care about. Jenny may be very fond of her nephew and very sorry for him in his desperate situation. She would rather please him and save him and his family from a time of great anxiety and misery, by doing something that is slightly underhand that will not hurt anyone, least of all her uncle who will never know. At a pinch she tells herself she could always put the money back into his account herself, borrowing it from the bank.

But taking on the power of attorney and running her uncle's affairs is a form of trust. She has promised, by signing the forms, to care for his money in his interests. She is simply not free to use it as if it were her own account. If John and Peg pay in cash and avoid tax, then society is a tiny fraction closer to a state where we cannot trust financial business transactions and bribery is a way of life. Here, Jenny's act in using her uncle's money would be another step in the same direction. But none of us thinks it realistic to see our small actions as part of a greater whole. Our sense of duty to obey the law has been weakened by various changes that we talked about in the last chapters, and so it is harder to do the right thing and face the disappointment and misunderstanding of others.

Jean is 35 years old, reasonably happily married with four children, aged 12, 10, 8 and 6. In one single act of desperately regretted folly, she had intercourse with the husband of a friend. She is now in early pregnancy. Because Jean and the man she slept with are different racially, it will be obvious if the baby is his, with unthinkable consequences for so many people, including her children. She is desperate for an abortion.

Many people, and especially members of religious groups, are deeply and often passionately concerned about the working of the Abortion Acts. When there was no legal abortion, Jean's situation, terrible as it is, could only be resolved in another way. She would have been faced with the possibility of illegal abortion, with all the risks to her health and life that it entailed. The only other possibility would be full confession to her husband in the hope that he would be willing to reconstruct his life with her, at least for the sake of the children. But his relationship with her is not the only one threatened. He would know who the father was, and their relationship too would be damaged and maimed.

Once abortion becomes possible, it seems the easiest solution all round. Jean will not have to endure seeing so many others, as well as herself, hurt by her folly. The issue of abortion does not just involve the rights of those already born, however. The rights of the unborn should also be considered, and for many people the killing of the unborn for convenience's sake is no different from the killing of unwanted children. Jean will watch her children grow up. If she keeps in touch with the friend, and that will probably be very difficult, she will watch his children as well. The adults, and probably the children as well, will know the situation if Jean does not have an abortion. If she has an abortion, Jean will always know that there should have been another child, one whose life she stopped. The dilemma is not just hers; her doctor also has to weigh all these things. Governments can pass Acts of Parliament, but the awful choices are given to ordinary people.

As you read through these dilemmas, ask yourself whether there are other factors that we have not mentioned. How would you react yourself? What are the most important influences on your decision-making? If you can see a pattern in your own response, are you being guided by the rules, by the consequences, or by strong feelings? In the next chapter we will describe more of these brief scenes in people's lives. Many of them are taken from real life, but, of course, we are not able to cover every detail and sometimes there is a crucial fact missing that would sway the argument one way or another. However, in real life we do sometimes have to decide without knowing as much as we would like.

CHAPTER 12

Facing more problems

Sue and Rob's eldest daughter wants to come and stay for the weekend. (Their 14-year-old son is still at home.) Their daughter has a partner with whom she lives in her London flat. Sue and Rob are embarrassed and worried. Should they give the couple the spare double room? Should they put them in separate rooms? Should they explain what they decide, and in what way?

If Sue and Rob's daughter wants to come to stay, then she probably has a reasonably good relationship with them, and will not put them in this position. If she knows that they do not approve of unmarried couples living together, and that they will be concerned about the impression on her brother, she will assure them that she expects to be given separate rooms. What if she does not do this? Rob and Sue will then have to weigh up their desire to make a stand on marriage against their wish to maintain their relationship with their daughter. They have to ask whether there is a difference between casual partnerships and those that show all the commitment of marriage, and whether they can accept the young couple in that way.

David's mother of 89 may need an operation. He wants to say no, to allow her medical condition to take its course and to look after her in his own home. His sister, Frankie, is adamant that everything should be done to extend their mother's life.

Many people face difficult decisions as they grow old. We sometimes hear people reflecting that the modern generation do not look after their elderly relatives—comparing what happens now with past generations, or with kinship patterns of care in other countries. But we sometimes forget the great changes that have taken place in family structures, and at the same time we may have rather inaccurate pictures of the past. Two factors combine to present us with a situation that is different from those in the past and in other countries. We have far smaller families, and far less contact with those outside the nuclear family. We also live longer, with larger and larger numbers surviving into their eighties and beyond. Families used to be bigger 'widthways' in space, but smaller 'lengthways' in time. If the birthrate continues to fall, and more people choose not to have children, there will be families where a married couple could have all four grandparents, perhaps two great-grandparents, and several aunts to care for.

These changes in family size and shape are already putting pressure on the provision of care for handicapped and frail elderly people. Social services are asking how they should spend scarce resources on people over eighty, while the possibility of successful treatment for even extremely old people is growing all the time. David and his sister have to ask themselves some questions about their approach to their mother's operation. They may have reasons that need challenging by each other. They need to talk honestly with her medical carers. They also need to ensure that they are not riding roughshod over their mother's own wishes. Even if she is confused, her wishes should be considered. Too often the elderly are expected to do what they are told.

Every Sunday, Bill cajoles his three teenagers to go to church with him and their mother. It is a principle with him that families should do that kind of thing together and he is deeply threatened by their simmering rebellion. Miriam, his wife, finds the services dull and boring. Every now and again she pretends to have a headache and stays at home for an hour of peace and quiet. She cannot work out whether she should be honest and blow the whole charade apart, or go on supporting Bill and escaping with a white lie when she can.

Poor Bill! If he sloped off to the pub and took no interest in his family, he would be seen by some as a typical male of a certain kind, leaving the creation of family life to his wife. He is trying hard to make his family work, but he is doing so by telling them what to do and insisting that they do it. This goes against many of the underlying trends of our time. Unless parents are willing to discuss and to justify the conditions that they lay down for their children, they will frequently be ignored and disobeyed. When that happens, there is little that fathers or mothers can do, unless they escalate the confrontation and attempt sanctions that are very difficult to enforce.

If you wish to bring your children up in a way that goes against all the norms of their age group and the patterns of their peers, you probably need to buy a rural farmhouse before they are born, educate them at home, and ban a large proportion of the incoming media. Bill's children may have long passed the age at which you can insist that children do what, or go where, you ask. (Fortunately, school is compulsory!)

But there is also a growing rift between Bill, his wife and his children. Do the children sense that their mother is a reluctant participant as well? If so, he is increasing the damage to their family relationships. This family needs an honest, humble willingness to listen to each other, a willingness to allow the expression of strong feelings without resentment, and a desire to put aside self-interest and do things for the others' sake. This may be too difficult for immature teenagers, but they are not going to learn such attitudes unless their parents are willing to demonstrate them.

Tom has just started a new job as a middle manager in a complex engineering firm. Promotion has taken him, after six months, to another part of the country. He realizes that part of his responsibility is for a factory making equipment which is exported to overseas police forces. It includes electric cattle prods, shackles and various forms of handcuffs. He is very disturbed and wonders whether he should resign.

Dilemmas at work are not often as extreme as this one. There are certain industries where it would be difficult for anyone to work who is seeking to live a good and honourable life. These would include, for example, some parts of the entertainment industry, that involve the commercialization of sex, and parts of the media, that exploit gossip and rumour. For many, the problems presented are to do with the petty flouting of rules, the short cuts in accounting, and the management styles that exploit and bully employees. In management, many people face difficult choices as they seek to serve their firm and its senior directors with loyalty and at the same time be fair and honest with those working under them, and with rival companies. Resigning on principle from a job is not easy when the next job might be hard to find and there is a mortgage to pay and a family to support. Of course, Tom may find that if he discusses his problem with his bosses, they too have qualms and he may precipitate important changes of policy. There again, he may not!

Justin's wife has had multiple sclerosis for many years. Now very badly affected, she is living in a local Cheshire Home. Justin has recently met Sarah, through their local history club. His children are adults who have all left home. He would love to set up home with Sarah, since both are now in their fifties and feel very lonely. He does not know what to do.

When we marry, we promise someone that we will stay with them, love them and care for them whatever happens. Whether they are paralysed in a road accident on the day after the wedding, or become chronically ill 20 years into the marriage, the promise is the same. Most people nowadays hedge that promise with boundaries (although probably not consciously, at the moment when they are declaring the promise at the wedding). As we consider situations, perhaps of chronic illness, or where there is physical abuse, long-term neglect, childlessness, or some other unexpected hitch, we might all say that there are limits. Few people expect to carry on in a marriage in any circumstances, but leaving an abusive spouse is very different from leaving a helpless invalid. At the same time, it is hard to say that someone else should show supreme self-sacrifice when we ourselves are not in their position.

Sam and Jill work together in a small solicitor's office in a small town. They usually have lunch together. One Monday Sam tells Jill something that he has read in a letter in the office that morning. It concerns the private life of a family they both know. It is exciting and quite shocking information. Jill meets a fair number of people round town, at her evening class and at her squash club, who also know the family. That evening, as she sits having coffee after playing squash, she finds herself in the middle of a sentence broadly hinting at what she has learned. Half way through, she knows that she should not repeat it and that Sam should not have told her, but the excitement of passing it on and becoming the centre of attention are too much for her.

Much of human communication consists of telling stories about what we have been doing and what others are doing. Many of us live in several different worlds, of work, home and leisure. Often these worlds do not meet, and we feel free to relate the gossip of home at work with little chance that the story will get back to the original person. Because storytelling can be exciting, and because we do not like bores, we may well embroider it, or we may, as Jill is probably doing, not quite tell the complete story. She does not want to reveal the fact that she is passing on information gained in a solicitor's office, so she gives it a fuzzy touch.

Sometimes we do not really know what stories we should tell, which ones are common knowledge and which those involved are happy to have repeated. Jill should have stopped Sam in mid-track before he said anything substantive. Here in a small town, Jill is doing the kind of character assassination that troubles all of us about the media, especially newspapers with their coverage of celebrities and royalty. When does gossip stop being gossip and become a news item that needs to be broadcast? Is gossip a bad thing? We use the word 'gossip' to mean passing on tales about others that should not be repeated. Could we tell the same tale in two different ways, only one of which would be called gossip?

Kelly works in the office of a building society in a small town. Her grandfather works a farm on its outskirts. One Sunday lunchtime, her grandfather tells the family that he is going to plough the only remaining grassland meadow on the farm and plant flax. It is the only way he is going to make ends meet. The meadow has never been ploughed and is rich in plants and insects that used to be common all over the countryside. Kelly, who belongs to several environmental groups, becomes very angry. Her grandfather points out that her building society is backing a large housing development on another green-field site down the lane.

We are surrounded by environmental issues that make many of us very angry. We may feel that all that we love most is being destroyed around us. But the issues are not simple. Many want the right to roam freely on the wild and lovely moors and hills of this land. Others can see that the paths are being eroded and the pressure of too many people is destroying the very things they come to experience. The battle is often between big business, people's livelihoods and the costs of environmental care. Someone has to pay. Should Kelly's grandfather be paid to preserve the meadow? We have to make small decisions as we shop. Should we buy organic food? Should we boycott manufacturers whose environmental record is poor? How can we know? For many, the answer is to join organizations, as Kelly has, that will research and campaign for better care of the world.

Sandy and Hannah have been married for ten years. They have two children aged 6 and 4. Their relationship has steadily worsened over the past four years, and Sandy has had two affairs with women at work. He says that he still loves Hannah and wants to stay with her, but he cannot promise that an affair will not happen again. Hannah is unsure what to do. Many of her friends tell her that she should divorce him and make a new life for herself. She dreads being on her own and still enjoys Sandy's company. He is a devoted father, and is often more likely than she is to find things for them to do, and places to take them that stimulate and excite them. She dreads bringing the children up on her own. What should she do?

There will be many who sympathize with Hannah's position. One of the saddest consequences of such a situation is that the couple's friends will probably end up having to take one side or the other. The strong sense of betrayal may lead Hannah to want to cut her losses and leave Sandy, hoping that he may become really sorry and perhaps learn just how far he has mucked up all their lives. Nevertheless, the growing evidence that children with divorced and separated parents suffer consequences far into adulthood may make her grit her teeth and stay in the marriage. We have a huge responsibility for the children we bring into the world.

We have assumed too readily that children suffer more in a home where the adults are not happy together than with separated parents. Here is a situation where we will be driven by very strong emotions, and the desire to rationalize and find excuses for what we want to do can be very strong. Yet children do suffer when their parents split; they are more likely to show increased ill-health, poorer performance at school, more frequent mental illness and poorer adult relationships themselves than the children whose parents stay together. Of course these are averages and we can always tell ourselves that our children will be different. We will make an effort to see that they relate to both parents well. We know it can be done successfully. But the risks are huge and the regrets, if they come, are difficult to cope with. What should Hannah do?

PART TWO

Is there a Christian way to live?

CHAPTER 13

Is there a Christian way to live?

In the last two chapters we have looked at a range of situations in which people had to decide how to act. They had to make choices between different courses. They had to make up their minds about right and wrong. In books about moral decision-making, writers often look at particular issues. Those most frequently discussed are medical ethical issues, including abortion, euthanasia and genetic engineering. There is often a discussion about war and peace and whether war can be justified. Homosexuality and divorce also come up, as well as the right to strike and civil disobedience. In more recent books, the environment and business ethics are also included. These are very important issues and some of the stories in the previous chapters touch on them. However, many of us will not be challenged in these areas very often. It is important that we work out our position and think through these issues, even if we are not able to come to a firm conclusion. For many of us, though, the situations we are more likely to meet are those that are about gossiping, telling the truth, and adapting to the different standards of our children and changing attitudes to sex and marriage.

Would it have made any difference to the people in our stories if they had been Christians? Would John and Peg have chosen to obey the law, or to thank the builder for his kindness? Would Mary have stayed at home to look after her children and cook and clean? Would they all have been more likely to obey the rules? Would they have definitely paid their income tax? Definitely never left a spouse who was ill? Definitely never have committed adultery? Never slept with a partner unless they were married? Never have countenanced abortion, whatever the circumstances? Or would they be more likely to have seen love, kindness and care for others as the most important guide, and therefore done the soft and gentle thing, even if it meant breaking strong rules?

A decision to live as a Christian will mean that we have to assess and then accept or reject the authority of the rules and guidelines that we have acquired through our upbringing and schooling and experience, from our parents, our peers, our society and culture and our previous religious beliefs and background. We will need to find out exactly how being a Christian will change the way we make decisions and the kind of people we are.

Making our decisions and then acting on them does not end our problems, however. We do not make decisions independently, as if we had our own blank sheet to write our lives on. We are all enmeshed and tied up with other people and with our own past. We find ourselves in the middle of a problem that was created because we made wrong decisions yesterday, or because someone else acted in a way that affected us. We did not think hard enough before we spoke or acted. Humans do not simply need good guidelines. We also need a way of handling past mistakes. We need to know how to put things right after we have done the wrong thing. We need to know how to deal with guilt and regret, with bitter recriminations and with other people's damaged lives. We need to find a better way to live that not only helps us in the future but also reaches back into the past to put right, as far as is possible, the wrongs that have already been done. As well as the tools for making future decisions, we need the means to put right bad decisions from the past.

Of course, not all the choices we make are moral ones. We have to choose between different makes of car, between different courses at school or college. We have to decide on the colour of our bathroom and the length of our hair. We have to decide whom to marry and which job to apply for. There may be ethical factors in these choices. One car may be very large and use a great deal of petrol. One college may be very far from our parents, which may tempt us to accept the offer. Christians may need to pray about such choices and we may need to learn some home truths as we decide these things, but they do not all come into the arena of morals.

What are Christian ethics? How do ordinary people, including many Christians, answer this question? During World War I, the chaplains sent by the Church of England to the battlefront discovered things about the popular beliefs of ordinary men that surprised and shocked them. The chaplains were parish vicars and ministers who had conducted services in their churches but had not spent much time discussing matters of life and death with ordinary people. In the trenches, the immediate stark realities of war meant that soldiers were more than willing to ask deep and important questions about life and death, and goodness, and getting to heaven.

The chaplains saw that many of the men demonstrated traits of character that would not have been apparent in peacetime. They were deeply and sacrificially loving, they cared for each other, they wept and grieved over their losses, they showed patience and gentleness, great courage and endurance. But when the chaplains talked about Christian morality, the men did not see these traits as having anything to do with being a Christian. If asked to outline what Christian goodness was about, they would repeat a list of don'ts: 'Don't smoke, don't drink, don't swear, don't go with prostitutes'. As far as they were concerned, being a Christian was about not doing things that many of them took for granted as soldiers! The chaplains asked more questions and found that the vast majority of the men had been to Sunday school as children. There they had learnt simple Christian stories from the Bible and had been taught simple rules for life. But they left the church when they reached the age at which many of them had started work, at 12 onwards. They had never acquired an adult understanding of what Christianity was about. They saw the church as a spoilsport, a wet blanket.

That was a long time ago, but I suspect that there are people who still have that kind of idea in their heads about Christian goodness. Their view of Christian morality is that it is all about rules and regulations to stop people enjoying themselves—like the headteacher of a 1950s girls' school, who changed the uniform to brown stockings when black was fashionable, and back to black when brown was popular. Many who were brought up in the church through the last century felt that there was a disapproving glare coming from the church, as leisure increased, swimsuits became scantier, and films and television dominated spare time.

Other distorted impressions have prejudiced people against Christian morality. Some have seen it as not very manly, fine for women and children but too soft, forgiving, and submissive. Others have been brought up in a different tradition. They may have been to one of the more old-fashioned boys' public schools, with chapel once a week, where the traditions of the army, of service to one's country, of courage and a stiff upper lip, were seen as Christian virtues—where fighting the battle, manning the gun, and marching to do one's duty were the pictures of Christian right living.

Many today assume that the church is only concerned about sexual morals. The popular press and public opinion are only aware of the input of the church where issues of sexuality are concerned, and where it seems that the church is usually saying, 'Don't'. Above all, many are aware that the Christian churches speak with different voices and that arguments in the public media are sometimes between members of the same church.

The most common accusation brought against Christians and the Christian church is that of hypocrisy. They are accused of saying one thing and doing another. The only difference that can be seen between those inside and outside the church in terms of moral behaviour is that the people inside keep telling the people outside how to live, when they are just as bad themselves. This is a particularly difficult jibe for Christians to deal with. There are two ways of looking at this accusation of hypocrisy. The first is that Christians are not good people, but for-given people. They know they are just as likely to have made mistakes and acted wrongly as everyone else, but they have admitted these things, recognized that they were wrong and have sought forgiveness. They are not saying that they are good, but that they know they are bad!

But there is another side to the accusation of hypocrisy. Many people would probably work on the basis that if enough people keep on doing something that was considered wrong, then it ceases to be wrong. Morality changes as behaviour changes. This view is particularly true in the area of sexuality. Many people can see no reason at all why being sexually active is wrong unless it hurts others. If individuals want to do something that is enjoyable and gives great pleasure, why on earth shouldn't they go ahead? But the fact that a very large number of people, a majority perhaps, believe something does not necessarily mean that they are right. It is possible for a few far-sighted people to see the truth when everyone else is misled. We have to challenge the assumption that because everyone is doing something, this means it is right.

Being judgmental is another accusation that is made against Christians. It is quite difficult sometimes to state that doing something is wrong, and not sound as if we are blacklisting everyone who is doing it! Jesus told his disciples that they should not judge, and compared judging others to trying to remove a speck of dust from someone's eye, when there is a plank of wood in your own! But he didn't say that we should ignore the speck and the plank and pretend that they are not there. He said we should get rid of the plank so that we could see more clearly to remove the speck.

Christians also encounter problems because they live and worship within a culture that still thinks of itself as Christian in some ways. People will want to marry in church, even though they have lived together for some time. They can see no good reason why the church should have anything to say about this. They will want to bring their children for blessing or baptism, but will not take the promises that they make too seriously. They have their dead buried by Christian ministers in a Christian service, but do not feel that this carries any obligations to consider the claims of Jesus Christ. As the world changes round the church, so the gap between what the church teaches and what the world accepts may well grow so wide that it will eventually be clear to all that being a Christian means being very different.

Everyone who becomes a Christian already has a personal ethical system in place. We have looked at the array of different kinds of thinking that most of us bring to our choices of good living. We have mentioned laws, rules and principles, and for the Christian many of these will simply be affirmed as the ones common to humanity. We have mentioned role models and heroes, and Christianity has those. We have mentioned character and virtues, and Christianity lists those as well. We have looked at the underlying beliefs in our world, and Christianity introduces us to a new worldview. We have also mentioned the need for a way of putting past mistakes behind us, of dealing with the consequences of bad choices in the past, and Christianity deals with that as well.

We may have been a Christian for many years. We may have been brought up as one. We may be a new Christian who only walked into a church for the first time last week. We carry inherited and learned ways of behaviour. Now we have to ask how far we need to change. We have to take a long, hard look at ourselves and our assumptions. Some of us will need to change radically. Others may be affirmed in a lifestyle that already had all the hallmarks of a Christian understanding. Our starting point will be our trust in the living God, who walks beside us, guides and helps us. His tools will be the fellowship of other Christians in our local church, the Bible and the writings and traditions of the Christian past. Now we will look at these in more detail.

CHAPTER 14

Starting out as a Christian

If you are a Christian, a disciple of Jesus Christ, then you belong to a church. You may not be very keen on Sunday services. You may not have signed up to one of the big denominations. You may belong to a small local fellowship that meets in a local school, or even in the back room of a pub. But you cannot survive as a Christian believer and learn how to live as a Christian unless you are part of a Christian group. You may have belonged to a congregation for many years, perhaps a parish church in a village, or the Methodist church in the centre of a northern town, but you may not know the other members of the church very well. They may be neighbours, but your usual communication with them is to greet them on your way in and out of church on a Sunday, and to sit next to them and sing with them during the services. Many of us are attenders at churches but not part of a working, living fellowship.

It is very difficult to work out our Christian priorities on our own. It is hard to discover what the Bible is saying to us without consulting others and listening to what others think. Being a Christian is not a solo journey. Because we vary so much in our backgrounds and our personalities, and because we are prone to making mistakes and to allowing our prejudices to hide the truth from us, we cannot travel the Christian way on our own. The Bible expects us to work together with other Christians. The letters in the New Testament written to the first churches, were written to the whole church, not to individuals so that they could go away and read them behind closed doors. But in many parts of the church today, we simply never talk about our faith, our morals, our praying, with anyone else.

In the first book of the Bible, Genesis, there is a story of two brothers, Cain and Abel. Cain murders Abel, and afterwards God asks Cain where his brother is. Cain answers, 'I don't know. Am I my brother's keeper?'

The Bible implies that the answer to that question is, 'Yes'. We are responsible for each other and for the way we live. Of course, we are not to be bossy or interfering, nor to tell others what to do unless we have authority, but Christians are travelling together, and without each other they will frequently fail to make the right judgments between good and evil.

The Lord's Prayer is a communal prayer. It is not a prayer about me, it is a prayer about us. It is in the plural throughout. We pray for our daily bread. We are not simply praying for our own needs to be supplied, but for those of our fellowship, and beyond. The implications are that we cannot say that without accepting responsibility for others' hunger. We pray that we will not be led into temptation. We cannot pray that without making sure that we are not a source of temptation to others, and to do that we will need to be aware of others' weaknesses and to be our brothers' and sisters' keepers.

The first resource for Christians wanting to learn how to live a good life before the Lord is to be part of a group who can share their problems, discuss issues and pray for each other. We need to learn in community with others. It is the way that God works, building a fellowship of believers which becomes, through his Spirit, much more dynamic and effective than simply a gathering of individuals.

The Bible describes Christians in a number of different ways. Among other metaphors, they are disciples who follow a teacher, learners who sit at the feet of a guru, apprentices who go out to watch, work with and copy the ways of their leader, soldiers who arm themselves and go into battle following a commander, athletes who train in order to be fit for the race, pilgrims who travel towards the holy city. Christians do not learn the art of living a perfectly good life the moment they decide to follow Jesus. The learning process takes time, usually a lifetime.

The Christian life is a journey, a journey of discovery and learning. Christians have been rescued from a life without God, forgiven, dusted down and set on their feet. They have been put on the right tracks, given the right tools, and are following the right road. The way they walk this road, the way they relate to the people they journey with and meet along the way, the kinds of lives they live, are what ethics is all about.

The picture of the Christian life as a journey, during which we learn more about the road as we go, is a helpful one for many. It is a pilgrimage during which we mature, learn not to stumble, and watch out for the hazards along the way. For this walk, we need a guidebook with maps as well as company. In the next chapters we are going to look at the rules, principles and patterns of Christian ethical living. We will look at the Bible, our handbook; we will think about following the leader, guide and teacher, Jesus Christ and his Holy Spirit; and we will look at the implications of travelling with our fellow Christians, both the ones we relate to in the fellowship of a local church, and those who lived through the Christian centuries and have passed on to us their understanding of the journey and the best way to travel.

I wonder whether some of us, especially those who have been Christians for a long time, and who, in a way, function on automatic pilot much of the time, ever ask ourselves whether we have a Christian worldview and Christian lifestyle. We may have little idea what they would look like. Perhaps we should have a look at some examples of the kinds of inconsistencies that Christians live with, if they do not hear and obey Christian truths.

Jim is a banker. In church on Sunday, at communion, he hears Jesus' command to love your neighbour as yourself. On Monday he will be persuading a man with a small business to take out a loan. Jim has a quota to fulfil, although he knows that the man's business probably cannot carry the loan.

The man sitting next to Jim is one of the directors of a cigarette company. Together, they sing a hymn with the line, 'Through the world far and wide let there be light…' As cigarette sales fall in Europe, the director is battling for Third World markets where they can be sold more freely without having health warnings printed on the packets.

They sing, 'Bind us together in love'. The married couple sitting behind are in a state of horrified shock because their daughter has announced her engagement to a local boy whose parents came from the Caribbean and who is black.

Perhaps some of the characters we have met in previous chapters are sitting in the same church. Like us, week by week they hear passages from the Bible, the words of traditional hymns as well as new songs. They sing the psalms, and say the prayers that are set for that day. They look up at banners on the wall, or at stained-glass windows. Maybe our old friends, John and Peg, hear Jesus' words, 'Render to Caesar the things that are Caesar's'. Joan, who disliked her colleague enough to let her battery run flat, might see engraved on a window, 'Love your enemies and pray for those who persecute you'. Jim, who is thinking of paying a bribe, might read in Proverbs, 'Better to be poor and honest than a rich person no one can trust'.

When we hear, 'Honour your father and mother,' or 'I was in prison and you visited me', do we apply these words to ourselves? The charge of hypocrisy is sometimes not far from the mark. We can hear so much that should be guiding us in how we should live and warning us how to avoid some of the pitfalls in today's world. All too often, though, we do not really hear it or take it in and allow it to change the way we live. We may be committed Christians established in a local Christian group. But where do we go from there? If we are in the position of these Christians, and do not know how to apply much of what we hear in church to our own lives, then we may need to start up a discussion group so that we can use the resources of the others in the fellowship to explore the dilemmas and situations that have already been described in this book.

CHAPTER 15

Christian ethics: is love the only way?

Christian writers have long debated and argued over what shape Christian morals take. How does God tell us what we should do and not do in order to live good lives? Human beings change over the years— their cultures change—and we have seen how confusing we can find all the different ways of working out how to act. If God is the same for ever, eternally good and true, then surely his laws of right and wrong will also always be the same and will not change. Writers use the word 'absolute' to describe such rules that never change over time and place. If these rules exist, what are the absolutely true laws and where do we find them? Some writers have argued that we can work them out from the way humans and human society works. Others have said that we can be misled by our own thinking; we can misread the world round us. We have to listen to God, and not ourselves. They point out that God has indeed spoken to us and told us his laws, and they are written for us in the pages of the Bible. We should accept the authority of the Bible and not try to work it all out for ourselves.

The desire to have unchanging, absolute laws that should never be broken, corresponding to the unchanging nature of God, is very strong. Does the Bible give us these? Can we simply read it and do what it says? We have already looked at some of the commands that are included in the Ten Commandments, one example of a list of God's laws. We have looked at murder and stealing, and seen that it is not possible to say simply, 'Do not kill,' and 'Do not steal'. Not all killing is murder, so we have to describe what murder means; and we have to work out exactly what activities we include under the heading of stealing. In the New Testament, Jesus extended murder to include being angry with a brother. He went on to extend and develop other Old Testament laws, teaching that the spirit, or principle, behind the law was more import-ant that the bare command itself. These laws about murder and stealing could be seen as God's minimum, only the beginning of a Christian moral position. Do we have to go further back to a more basic foundation for Christian ethics?

One very popular Bible reading is the extract from Paul's letter to the church at Corinth where he talks about love. He describes love as patient, kind, not envious, not proud, not rude, not self-seeking, not easily angered, keeping no record of wrongs, not delighting in evil, rejoicing in the truth, always protecting, always trusting, always hoping, always persevering. There is a great deal about love in the Bible. 'God is love' is a text that appears frequently in many forms from Victorian samplers to stained-glass windows. Why, then, some have argued, do we need masses of rules and regulations in lists like the commandments? All we need is love. We do not need any other ethical rule. If we act in love in all our dilemmas, then we will do the best, do what is right and good.

A number of writers have suggested that love is the one absolute rule. This seems to be backed up in the Bible, for when Jesus was asked to sum up all the Law of the Old Testament, he gave two commandments to love—the first to love God, and the second to love our neighbours as ourselves. Of course, there are many kinds of love. The Greek language in which the New Testament was written had several different words for the different kinds of love: *eros* for romantic love, *philia* for the love of friends, and *agape* for the kind of love that Jesus and Paul were talking about. This kind of love is unselfish, wishing the best for others. Because we love God and God is love, we then love others, as well as ourselves.

Some argue that as Christians we should have just this one absolute law, and they give examples of the way such a law would work. All other rules can and should be broken if love demands it. A frequently quoted example describes a wartime situation in which you have fugitives hiding in the attic, and enemy soldiers come to the door and ask if you are hiding anyone. You know that they will kill the fugitives. Do you lie? Here, love says that of course you lie. Lying is not an absolute, but love is. The truth does not have to be told if something worse than lying will happen. Or a man is trapped in a burning crashed plane without hope of rescue. He begs to be shot before the flames reach him. If you have a gun, do you do what he asks?

These kinds of extreme situations very rarely occur, of course. But even in the more ordinary scenes that we looked at in chapters 11 and 12, we can see that a rule of love sometimes solves the dilemma, especially if you specify love for as many people as possible. Jean who is pregnant might decide, in love, to have an abortion because there is no other way to love all the people involved, including herself.

But there are problems with taking love as the only guide. We have to ask first of all what kind of love we are talking about. Will we know exactly what *agape* love, selfless love, is in any situation? We looked at the dilemma faced by Hannah, whose husband was unfaithful to her but did not want to end the marriage. Would love mean that Hannah would simply put up with his behaviour and keep her family intact? Some argue that in such a situation Hannah should show 'tough love', confronting Sandy with what he has done and excluding him from the marital home —that she is not loving properly if she condones what he has done.

Some parents smother their children with love, demanding their gratitude and sometimes seeking to keep them at home well into their adult years. Is that *agape* love?

We cannot trust ourselves to know fully what love requires. We may be driven by such strong emotions, that we call 'love', that we cannot see the way clearly. Parenting involves loving children, but even in caring for our offspring we do not always know what is the best in love. Parents who have had very sick children know how difficult decisions can be when a child needs long and distressing treatment.

Nor can we know all the people who need our 'love' when we have to decide what to do. John and Peg with the conservatory might think that they should 'love' their builder and give him cash. But if this undermines good business relationships, and begins a slide into tax avoidance by large numbers of people, then in love for the many, they should insist the full payments are made.

Love as a sole guide is too general. We still have to ask what we should do. Saying that we should do the loving thing is almost the same as saying we should do the good thing, and we are back where we started. What does 'good' mean? What does 'loving' mean? We still need the rules to guide us. Love as a guide to the future is too short-term. We may know what will happen in the next year, but we cannot tell what effect our actions will have in twenty years.

Love as an absolute on its own does not work. Jesus told us that the first commandment is to love God, the second to love our neighbour; but he did not leave these to stand on their own. He developed them by saying, 'If you love me, you will obey what I command' and, 'All the Law and the Prophets hang on these two commandments'. It is not that all the other laws are scrapped, but rather that we love God and our neighbour through obeying the rules and laws God gives us. But knowing that love is the important principle can form a good basis when we start to work our way out of a dilemma. It will help us to assess the rules that may apply. It will help when we can see two important rules in conflict—telling the truth or saving someone's reputation, for example.

The Gospel writer John tells a story about Jesus. A woman was brought to him who had been caught in the act of committing adultery. The lawyers who brought her knew their law, and pointed out that the penalty was death. Jesus did not say that the law's punishment should or should not be carried out. He suggested that any one of them who had not committed any wrong should be the one to start killing her. One by one they all melted away. Jesus was acting in love, but he was also acting justly. The lawyers were not interested in obedience to the law and doing the right thing. They were only interested in putting Jesus into a difficult situation. Moreover, they had caught her in the act, but they had not brought her male partner along as well. They were not interested in justice.

For weak humans, love does not work as a principle on its own without reference to other principles and rules. Christian writers on ethics have argued that love and justice together can go a long way to guide us as we work out how to live the good life. One of the Old Testament prophets said that God has shown us what is good: 'To act justly and to love mercy and to walk humbly with your God'. We need justice, mercy or selfless love, and especially humility, because none of us ever gets it completely right.

Even though, for humans, love cannot work as our guiding principle on its own, it is still in fact the only law. But the love which is the only law is not just anything we happen to call love. It is supremely the love embodied in the cross of Jesus, the love of God. We can begin to recover the meaning and the power of love only by insisting that love is interpreted completely and fully in the story of Jesus and his sacrificial death.

CHAPTER 16

Knowing the Bible

Imagine that all our characters, whose stories we have looked at in this book, happened to live in the same town, and happened to turn up in the same Christian fellowship. Together they worshipped, prayed and got to know each other. Then as they began to ask questions about living as Christians, and listened to the teaching of their church leaders, they would perhaps bring their problems into the open to seek answers as they prayed and talked together. Some of their problems would be so personal that they might only share with one or two trusted friends, but they might still ask more general questions that would contribute to their understanding of the way forward.

Above all, they would need to be able to bring the Bible, and all it contains, into their discussions. Without knowing its contents well, they would be floundering, half-remembering a text, recalling a parable, but not quite sure how to apply it; perhaps remembering a rule their mother taught them and wondering whether it was in the Bible or not. As new Christians, they would need to start on a basic programme of getting to know the scriptures. In the groups of Christians learning how to live together, there would need to be those whose knowledge of the Bible was thorough enough to be a resource for the whole group.

Reading and praying over the Bible in Christian community is our best basis for living the good life, for living as the Lord wishes, in obedience to him. But for many of us it is not easy to arrive at the point where we know it well enough to use it with discernment and skill. We may accept its authority, knowing that in it we will find all we need to know about ourselves, our God and what he requires of us, but we do not know how to go about applying it to all the situations of our daily lives.

There is a problem. Popular biblical knowledge has declined. Our friends who have newly joined a church may have only the sketchiest understanding of how the Bible is put together, how the Old and New

Testaments relate to each other or when it all happened in history. They may have read very little of it in school and never opened a Bible since. The ones they did read were in old English. They can read a light novel, but are totally daunted by the length and small print of most Bibles. They simply have to start from scratch. Most adults joining a church do not expect to have to go back to Sunday school! If we lead busy lives, the suggestion that we spend even half an hour a day reading the Bible, reading some notes on the passage and praying over what we have learnt, seems a lot to ask. Yet without these kinds of discipline, knowledge of the Bible will fall away even further.

The Bible input in the Sunday services that the new Christians will attend—readings, songs and hymns and a talk—will begin to give a flavour of the Bible story and will build the first blocks in their understanding, but that is simply not enough, nor will it happen fast enough to give them adequate tools to obey the Lord in all the different situations where they have to make choices. To learn to be thoroughly Christian in our thinking takes hard work and discipline. There is no escaping from that. Disciplined and time-consuming application to the Bible does not fit very well into modern lifestyles. This is one of the greatest challenges to living a good life.

The Bible uses an immense variety of teaching to tell us how to live. It is not simply a list of commands and rules, although it does have some of those, with the best-known concise summary in the Ten Commandments. It also has detailed and precise guidelines in the Mosaic law telling the people of Israel how to organize their daily lives: what to do if they find a neighbour's animal wandering through their land, how to treat people who are in debt to them, how to sow their crops. There are short, pithy sayings and proverbs: 'The greedy bring trouble to their families'; 'Pride goes... before a fall'. These are not laws as such, but wise comments on the consequences of behaving in certain ways.

There is poetic reflection on life: 'I saw that all labour and all achievement spring from man's envy of his neighbour. This too is meaningless, a chasing after the wind.' There is political and social challenge: 'You trample on the poor and force him to give you grain... You oppress the righteous and take bribes and you deprive the poor of justice in the courts... Hate evil, love good, maintain justice in the courts.'

There are the parables of Jesus. The story of the good Samaritan is told to answer the question, 'Who is my neighbour?' Jesus was quoting the Old Testament when he said that the second great command was to love one's neighbour as oneself; the command appears first in Leviticus 19 in a rather disconnected list of commands, which include instructions about sleeping with slave girls, clipping off the edges of beards and not using dishonest weights and measures. Jesus' questioner wanted to know who was his neighbour. Most people reading the command in the Old Testament would gather that it referred to one of their own people —a member of the community in which they lived, their own kin, household, clan or tribe. Of course, the Jewish law required Israelites to treat those not of their own kind—the strangers who lived among them—with love as well.

In the story of the good Samaritan, Jesus tells of a Jew who is mugged and badly injured on a journey. Two religious leaders pass by where he is lying on the roadside and avoid him. Finally a Samaritan, one of a people despised and looked down upon by the Jews, takes pity on him and rescues him. At one stroke Jesus makes us face all the parochialism, all the nationalism, all the ethnic cleansing, hatred and xenophobia of the ages, and he tells the questioner that the despised stranger, the hated foreigner, the smelly drunk, the one with the embarrassing handicap, could be doing better at loving their neighbours than the ones who thought they were good. There is no one who is not a neighbour.

There are stories in the Bible of heroes who are brave and good, but who also do terrible things. There are examples of bad relationships, and instructions on how to live in families. There are bloodthirsty battles in the Old Testament and Jesus saying, 'Love your enemies' in the New. How do we put all these things together? How do we use all this variety to make ordinary decisions today?

We cannot read all these different styles and types of writing in the same way. We cannot simply assume that we will do what it says. That may be the way to handle straight commands, but even those have to be worked on. 'Do not covet' is not easy to apply without a lot of thought and analysis of what 'covet' means in our own lives. We have to work out what any passage is saying, first to the original hearers, then to us. We then have to relate that passage to other passages which deal with a similar rule in a different way, and see how they modify each other. Because the Bible comes in such different styles of literature—

history, law, story, poetry, song, letter, parable, vision and dream—this is a challenging and exciting process.

The Bible was written at particular times and by people living in particular societies and cultures. This also makes it challenging and interesting to work out how the Bible applies to our daily lives. The social relationships of a rural agricultural society are not easily transposed to our modern world. The Bible says that when you are harvesting in your field and overlook a sheaf, you are not to go back and get it. Or, when beating the olives from your trees, you should not go over the branches a second time. Instead, you should leave what remains for the strangers, the fatherless and the widows. At first glance we can understand the principle behind these commands. We know that we cannot easily copy them, even if we own an orchard, but we can see what they mean: be generous; don't be a miser; don't keep your good fortune to yourself, give it away; watch out for those who suffer misfortune.

It is easy to see how we apply some of the commands, but not all the ethics of the Bible are as easy to translate into modern terms. As an example, we could take one chapter in the Old Testament. Leviticus 19 has 37 verses, beginning with the command, 'Be holy because I, the Lord your God, am holy.' It includes some of the Ten Commandments, but not in any particular order. 'Respect your mother and father... Don't make idols of cast metal... Do not steal. Do not lie.' It includes a passage about harvesting and leaving some of the crop behind for the poor and the stranger. It has commands we can all immediately see are applicable for all societies. 'Do not deceive one another... Do not defraud your neighbour... Do not hold back the wages of a hired man overnight... Do not put a stumbling-block in front of the blind... Do not turn to mediums or seek out spiritists.' 'Do not ill-treat foreigners who are living in your land. Treat them as you would a fellow-Israelite' (GNB). 'Rise in the presence of the aged, show respect for the elderly.' It says that doing these things is part of our service to God.

But there are other laws and commands that are not so easy to translate for ourselves. 'Do not mate different kinds of animals. Do not plant your field with two kinds of seed. Do not wear clothing woven of two kinds of material... Do not cut your bodies for the dead or put tattoo marks on yourselves.' Is the principle behind these that we should respect the natural world, including our own bodies? Could we use these verses, together with other passages, in the debate about changing the genetic make-up of plants or the morality of feeding cattle with slaughterhouse leftovers?

How do we decide which of these verses in this one chapter are very important and which ones may not be so relevant to us? In the middle of the chapter, there is one verse which reads, 'Do not seek revenge or bear a grudge against one of your people, but love your neighbour as yourself. I am the Lord.' Jesus took one phrase out of this verse, turned it into the second most important commandment, and in so doing extended its meaning. Loving your neighbour was no longer the alternative to bearing a grudge against somebody from one's own people, one's clan or tribe. In the parable of the good Samaritan, Jesus extended 'neighbour' to mean anyone who needed our help, and further made the point that the proud should be prepared to accept the neighbourliness of the despised. That gives us the clue that we need to read the Old Testament rules through the eyes of the New Testament. This is the way in which reading the Bible as a whole can help us avoid taking single passages out of context and applying them in inappropriate ways.

Looking at this chapter from Leviticus, we have been starting with the Bible and asking how we can apply it to life. The other side of this exercise is to start with our problem, taking it into the biblical text to see how the scripture can help us. Yet many of our dilemmas are simply not dealt with in the Bible, because they are products of our modern world. How do we take questions about abortion, genetic engineering, paying taxes, and find out how the Bible can help us think them through?

Some issues will be more difficult than others. Why is polygamy wrong when so many of the Old Testament men of God had several wives? Does the Bible permit divorce? If it does, how do we argue that men and women should be able to divorce each other on equal terms, when the Bible almost always refers to men divorcing women? Does the Bible condone slavery? Many in the past have argued that it does. Slave owners who were Christians said that the Bible permitted it. Most people nowadays would say that the implications of the references to slaves and slavery in the New Testament, and the underlying principle that all people are equal before God, lead the enquirer to accept that human beings cannot own each other and that the Bible does teach that slavery is wrong.

Sometimes, new ways of reading the text have led to new understandings of the way it teaches us to live. Theologians from Latin America and Africa and some women theologians have pointed out that the Bible has almost always in the past been interpreted by white middle-class men. Many have been blind to the Bible's message about poverty, and about racial and gender equality. We can be very biased as we read, hearing the words saying what we want them to say.

This might all sound as if knowing what the Bible says about morals is simply too difficult. But it is crucial that we study it together with other Christians, pooling our knowledge, sharing our insights and, above all, being led by the Spirit of truth. We believe that earnest seeking after truth, with a willingness to obey, is honoured by God, who leads us into truth. Our side of the task is to make the effort to become familiar with the Bible so that, together with others, we learn how to bring our problems and confusions under its authority.

Reading the Bible gives us rules and regulations but it also gives us principles that we apply in new situations; and underlying all that, it fundamentally changes our understanding of the world, so that we begin to think biblically and have a biblical worldview. We now turn to considering a Christian worldview and how such a view helps us to deal with ethical issues.

CHAPTER 17

Living in a good creation

How does the Bible teach us to view our world? We all understand reality and interpret ourselves as humans in a certain way. Our understanding of the social and natural world in which we live plays a crucial part in working out how to live, what is right and wrong and what kind of a person we want to be. This idea is not always easy to grasp. Our view of the world is not part of our conscious thinking. It is something we take so much for granted that we do not often question our basic attitudes, unless we come across someone who thinks very differently.

It may help to give one example of how this works. There are parts of the world where people have a very strong sense of fate. They believe that what happens to them was bound to happen because of things they have done in the past. It is the will of the gods. There is no point in trying to change things, or to get out of a situation. It was ordained and there is nothing they can do about it but accept it with resignation.

The underlying attitude of most people in the West is very different. They have an expectation that difficulties should be sorted out, that they should be able to find a cure or a solution—that humans should make an effort to rescue each other, to resuscitate, to make things better. Of course there are always variations. People differ in their reactions to life, but there is a tendency for groups of people, cultures with similar religious beliefs, to have the same basic underlying attitudes to what happens.

Imagine two small farmers, each living in a house with their family, surrounded by their fields and their grazing animals, one in Asia, the other in Western Europe. A terrible storm approaches, the river is rising, flooding is threatened. They may well react in very different ways if they have the two different attitudes to life we have outlined above. One farmer may make a great effort to prevent the floods reaching his land and that of his neighbours. Although the task is almost hopeless, he may mobilize all able-bodied people, make masses of sandbags and attempt to raise the levels of the dyke walls. The forces of nature are to be fought and defeated. The other farmer may also see that there is almost no chance of preventing the catastrophe, but he also sees it as inevitable, as a fate that was written into his life story from his birth. To accept, to endure and then to start again is the way to come through.

If these farmers lose their farms and their livestock to the waters, one of them may feel guilty that he did not do enough, could not pile enough sandbags into the banks of the river, did not get his cows to the highest point in time. Thinking in this way, he might drive himself to despair. Although the other farmer may have done far less to protect his land, he may be more inclined to accept the blow as his fate and not blame himself.

How should those of us view it all who want to understand God's world through God's eyes? There are several possible outlines that would describe a Christian worldview, but I want to suggest one that a number of Christian writers have drawn up. This one focuses on the four most important points in the history of God's relationship with the world—creation, the fall (the point when evil entered the world), redemption (Jesus' death and resurrection), and the end, the time when God will bring everything to its final conclusion. These events form the basis of the Bible story, pull together a great deal of the biblical material and help us to see how it determines our thinking about right and wrong.

The first crucial belief describes how the world as we know it came about, that is, creation. To say that God made the world is only the beginning. Many people would claim this as their belief but what it actually involves does need spelling out. God existed before there was anything else, and he created the universe and everything that is, out of nothing.

At the back of many people's minds as they read this is an incomplete understanding about who God is. They have a mental picture of a powerful force, unknowable—perhaps thinking that this 'force' is worshipped by lots of people all over the world in different ways and under different names. They might add on the idea of God as Father, Jesus Christ and the Holy Spirit later. But this is not what the Bible says. We cannot simply decide for ourselves what God is like. The Bible has told us who he is. The God who created the world is the Trinitarian Christian God, Father, Son and Holy Spirit and there is no other. The Bible tells us that all things were made through Jesus. Many people use the word 'God' very loosely, but when Christians use the word, they should be talking about, as Paul often put it, the God and Father of our Lord Jesus Christ. It is he who made the universe, space, time and all that is.

There is another misunderstanding, and that is that God made the universe and then just set it in motion—winding it up, as it were—and that all the laws of nature, physics and chemistry, evolution and all the developments of social and economic human life simply progressed and produced the world as we know it, with God as a disinterested onlooker. The Bible teaches that God is the ongoing sustaining power behind everything that happens. He is involved in the universe at every level and without his undergirding love it would all collapse into a black hole. These two truths—that God is separate from creation, existed before it and created it all; and that he sustains it and is the force and power within it—are both very important. There are those who believe one of these truths and not the other.

The Bible then goes further and tells us that the universe that God made was good. God took delight in what he had made and enjoyed it. God's final act of creation at the beginning of the world was the making of a human being. God made humans male and female, he made them in his 'image', and he thought they were very good, too. This means that we are like God in ways that make us different from all the rest of creation. This likeness has been described in many different ways and there have been arguments about exactly what parts of human nature are included in the image of God. For our purposes here, it is important simply to recognize that humans have been set apart by God to relate to him in a way distinct from any other creature.

In addition, God has given us humans a unique role in the world we inhabit. We are his stewards, responsible for the day-to-day running of our whole environment. It is not ours to do with as we like; we are not bosses, lords with the power to destroy, but carers, gardeners and nurturers.

This doctrine of creation, with God as creator and sustainer of a good creation, and humans made in the image of God to be stewards of creation, has important consequences for ethics. As we have already implied in the last paragraph, our purpose in being placed in this world is to care for it. This means that much of the recent concern about the environment is an important change of view over the past decades and one that Christians should be part of. Growing numbers of people belong to organizations that care for the natural world, and others form pressure groups to fight environmentally damaging new proposals. These people are all acting ethically within a Christian view of creation.

This view should affect Christian attitudes to many of the issues about protecting the wild parts of the world, and preventing the extinction of animals and plants. But it also affects our attitude to issues about adequate provision of food and water for human communities, and questions about the use of pesticides, and building dams. These issues are more complicated, and we sometimes have to decide between preserving existing environments, and providing a reasonable standard of living for human communities. God has given us far more than the land to farm for food, however. Every human activity—mining for coal or gold, working out how to use nuclear power, genetically altering tomatoes so that they don't go soft, taking out hedgerows to make larger fields, using whitener when we wash our clothes, building golf courses on farm land—all these are issues that require thoughtful consideration in the light of the full Christian doctrine of creation. We are required to look after and not destroy, to husband and not waste, to use with restraint and pass on to our children the world we have been given.

We are only just beginning to think through the issues involved in our treatment of animals. Should we eat them? Hunt them? Farm them? If we accept that we have the right, as stewards of creation, to do all these things, then what is our responsibility in the way these things are done? Can we say that Inuit people in the Arctic can hunt, but people in Devon should not? If we say this, then we have to work out a good answer when we are asked to justify this difference. Should we farm in such a way that the animals we eat, milk and shear live reasonable lives? All of these very topical issues also need understanding within the context of our doctrine of creation.

This created world is more than simply the world of nature, the material world around us. Creation also includes human beings, not just as farmers and carers of the environment, but also as social creatures. God has made us social people, and we create cultures, societies and groups of enormous diversity. We develop law and government, family structures and kinship patterns; we build cities and communications networks; we sing and we dance. All these areas are part of God's creation too, and if individuals are made in God's image, so too are our joint enterprises: the creation command to be stewards extends to these areas as well. As Christians, we should not withdraw but work for God in the world, to bring about the Kingdom of God, to seek justice and truth, to fight the abuse of power, to restore human dignity, to bring reconciliation and reconstruction where we can. We should not turn our back on the communities round us. There too we need to be involved, in as critical and discerning a way as we care for the environment, joining with people of goodwill who may not be Christian, to change every part of our world into the image of God.

Our doctrine of creation has implications for the way we treat each other. If we believe that every human being is made in the image of God, then we must view human beings as having great worth. Each one has the potential to be like God; all are of infinite worth to him. Humans are different from all the rest of the animal world. Of course humans are animals, and their physical, mental and often social characteristics obey the same laws as those of the rest of the mammals in creation. Our DNA is very similar to that of chimpanzees! But God has breathed his Spirit into us, he has made us in his image, and we have to treat each other in ways that recognize that truth. We cannot treat people as expendable; we cannot enslave them, or torture them; we cannot use them in experiments against their will, or get rid of them because they are simply in the way. If they cannot care for themselves, then others must care for them as children of God.

Sadly, the good and beautiful world that God created at the beginning of time has been spoilt, and knowing that gives us another building brick in our Christian worldview.

CHAPTER 18

Living in a spoilt world

We are perhaps not overcome enough by the wonder and goodness of the world. It is not just the natural world that should amaze us, although that is overwhelmingly and breathtakingly wonderful. You don't have to think very hard to remember being moved by creation. Built into it, there are so many enormous and glorious surprises—the first inkling of what birds of paradise are like in a wildlife film; a squirrel who has just tumbled off the bird table trying to get the nuts; the yellow of the first primroses of spring. And then there is all the incredible inventiveness of humans who have been given the ability to recreate with all the materials, energies and processes that are available to us and are awaiting our discovery.

The world of human society also has its glorious surprises—reading a novel, listening to music, singing in a choir, talking to friends, being loved by children and grandchildren, sex, food, sport, the immense pleasure of suddenly understanding something that had proved diffi- cult, poetry and even politics—Nelson Mandela becoming President of South Africa, the Berlin Wall coming down.

The world is still so good, but it is also torn and twisted. For every good thing I have mentioned above, there is a time and a place when it has been spoilt or destroyed, wantonly, cruelly, with evil intent, or with absence of mind. From the musician who goes deaf to the child who dies, from pornography to urban dereliction, from war to commercial exploitation, from stolen food aid to technology to poison and kill.

It is this permeation of the good creation with evil, into every joint and tissue, that means we have a difficult task to be upright, good and righteous in our world. Even so, the purpose of our lives in one sense is to promote the good, to affirm it and take delight in it wherever we find it, and to fight the bad, turn away from it and to lessen its impact on human lives and their world.

This underlying view, that everything is good but spoiled, is extremely important. It has implications for the way we handle many of the difficult situations we meet. It should influence the way we react to the treatment of human beings. We recognize that humans are made in God's image, that they are potentially like him and are of infinite worth to him. But they are also spoiled—not just because they do wrong and can sometimes be evil beyond ordinary imagining, but also because they are spoilt through no fault of their own. Around us we see physical and mental disability; traumatic injury through accident and ill-treatment; malnutrition and social breakdown through war, famine and natural disaster, emotional and mental damage through bad parenting and abusive relationships. All these things mean that, frequently, humans are only a faint and marred image of God. No one is free of the handicap of being part of a fallen creation, but even so, we should never count another human being as being of little importance because they are damaged. We are bound in common humanity, created by God, to treat them all with love and justice.

This is why the image of human beings that is portrayed in the media, in magazines and in advertising, is sometimes cruel and damaging. The message presented is that the ideal person is young, slim, suntanned, confident, beautiful and sexually attractive. Anyone who does not match up is second- or third-rate. Self-confidence is sapped. Disability is despised. Age is the final misfortune. Even those who are aware of the effect of such images find it hard to see beyond the outward appearance to the inward goodness. Even US presidential candidates are more likely to be elected if they are taller than their opponents!

The truth that everything is awry, tainted with evil, not quite what it should be, should lead us all to a deep humility. Even though we may have a brilliant mind, even if we are philosophers of world renown, we have to acknowledge that our intellects, our rationality, are also fallen. We may be able to achieve amazing things, but at the end we have to say, 'I am only human, I have to listen to others and know that I just may have made a mistake.'

Our ethical systems in every culture, in every society, will also be both good and bad, like everything else. Indian custom in earlier centuries said that wives should love their husbands, but considered that this love should be expressed by widows throwing themselves into their husbands' funeral pyres. Today we agree that babies should be wanted and loved, but some say that if they are not, it is right to get rid of them before they are born. We value and long for romantic love to carry us into marriages that are heaven on earth, but when we feel that way again with someone else, we move on and break promises. When we meet such mixed-up ethics, as Christians we will need to work out what we should oppose and confront, what we should affirm and support, and also, in some areas, where we have to learn to disagree with other Christians.

This kind of attitude is important because Christians do argue about morality. There are arguments that have gone on since the Bible was first put into its present form over exactly what it says about a number of topics. There are areas where devout Christians disagree, and in these areas of disagreement it is important to remember that we are not perfect.

Fran was part of a group in a local church, running a course in parenting. Many new mothers, as well as one father, had come along, all anxious to know that others had the same problems as them. They were using a range of material for group work and the discussions had been warm and reassuring. However much they expressed concern about some of the problems they faced, they agreed on the principles of loving, responsible childcare. Then one week a young American woman joined the group. She told them that she came from a large church in Texas which had also begun classes in parenting, but the classes had fallen apart because there was a deep difference of opinion about what good parenting meant. It was seen as a key issue in fighting social ills by breaking the cycle of poorly brought-up children bringing up their own delinquent offspring. But the class had divided into two opposing camps.

There were those who were firm believers that the Christian way was strongly authoritarian and that discipline, and often physical discipline, was the key. They believed that children were sinful and that unless they were trained to obey (if necessary by force), they would go astray as adults. They would quote Proverbs, 'Do not withhold discipline from a child; if you punish him with the rod, he will not die... Folly is bound up in the heart of a child, but the rod of discipline will drive it far from him.'

The other group were aghast that such a view should emerge from studying the Bible. In their turn they argued that parents should teach their children what God's loving kindness and patience mean, by modelling those values in their childcare. They should teach by action that Jesus loved sinners, that God's forgiveness was a free gift of grace, and that an emphasis on discipline, training and obedience gave an entirely false picture of what parents and, by extension, God, were like.

Christians disagree, and these Christians are disagreeing because they are each emphasizing one side of the goodness and fallenness of human beings in creation. All those in authority, with power of any kind over others—parents, teachers, judges, police, bosses and governments—have to be aware of their own limitations, their own tendency to err, and should take that into account as they work out how to act.

There are a host of other areas where Christians have to work out together a way through differences like the one above. In the past, some of the most intractable issues have been war and pacifism; the observance of the Sabbath; the position of women in society, the home and the church; and slavery. Slavery is no longer an everyday issue for Christians. Almost everyone agrees that it is immoral, although some of the economic arguments of the 18th and 19th centuries are used today in the debate over issues of fair trading and the low pay of developing world plantation workers, picking bananas, sugar cane and tea.

A small church in South Africa in the late 1980s had to face issues of war and peace when the sons of church families were called up to serve in the army. A few of the young men were sure that they should not serve in an army that was being used repressively against fellow South Africans. As Christians they were conscientious objectors. One of them was sent to prison. Most of the rest of the young men in the church felt that as citizens they were called to do their duty to the state, and they accepted their call-up papers.

How does a fellowship handle such a situation? After talking and praying about it, and battling not to let the divide, which was deep politically and socially, pull them apart, the families of the young decided that they would take responsibility for all the young men. They would honour them in doing what their consciences demanded. The families of young men who were serving in the army would write to the one in prison, and the family of the one in prison would communicate with the ones in the army. They would keep them in touch with home, send them parcels, meet regularly to pray for them, and encourage the young men to accept that sometimes we do differ, but we differ in love and learn in humility from each other.

The battles about the Sabbath are mostly over. Some who grew up in Christian homes before the 1950s will remember them. For many, it was a sad and repressively boring day. The fourth commandment says, 'Remember the Sabbath day by keeping it holy.' It is the longest commandment, entailing a number of consequences if it is disobeyed. Trying to work out what that meant in practice, centuries after the day of rest had changed from the Sabbath to Sunday, entailed much bitter argument.

The discussion rumbles on about the rights and wrongs involved in relationships between men and women, whether in the workplace, the home or the church. And Christians disagree. The story of creation in Genesis, the first book of the Bible, tells us that here at the core of human relationships, the entrance of evil has created deep wounds, which we continue to live out in our daily lives. The battle about the roles of men and women is about justice, and about the pain of relinquishing authority and power, but it is also about accepting situations that we cannot change and not letting them make us bitter and resentful.

The Bible writes about many heroes of faith, and one whose story takes up many chapters in the Old Testament is King David. He is praised and honoured, seen not just as the ancestor of Jesus, but as a forerunner, foreshadowing some of the attributes of Jesus himself. He was a poet and a theologian whose psalms we still sing. But he was also a fallen human being, showing great weakness and failure in his relationships within the family, with wives and with his children, and thus causing huge problems for his country. The story of how his lust led him to adultery and murder is vivid and chilling, yet even from such moral failure as this he was able to find mercy, forgiveness and the chance to start again.

We know we will fail; we know that sometimes we will make the wrong decisions and do the bad rather than the good, the wrong rather than the right. We would be in despair if we had no way out, but like David we can find forgiveness and start again.

CHAPTER 19

Can we make things better?

We have already included in this book a dozen or so examples of individuals facing moral decisions. In almost all of them, those individuals are at the point of decision, at the crossroads where they can choose from two or more directions to go. They have to decide which one is right and which is wrong, or which is better and which is worse. But many of us have already gone down a particular road. Sometimes it may not be a particularly bad one, but we are still wishing we had chosen differently. We can now see only too clearly the consequences, and they fill us with foreboding. What do we do then? What kind of choices are left to us?

Darren's job took him all over the world. He was frequently away from home for long periods of time. When he came home, it took time to relax into his family's way of life. The children, especially the two younger ones, were always difficult and demanding for several days after he came back. Stressed and sometimes too tired to care, he began to watch the pornography that was easily available in his hotel rooms. He became addicted, even wishing he could get away from home to the anonymity of a hotel. One August he came home after three weeks away. He was tired and irritated, his irritation made worse by his wife's attempts to make him feel welcome and loved. He lost his temper and, in a shouting match, admitted his addiction in accusations that were brutal and obscene. He drove away from home and sat in his car down a quiet lane. He was totally appalled and ashamed. The enormity of what he had become, and what he had done to himself and his family, overwhelmed him. Was there a way out?

Books on ethics are almost always about how we make decisions and not what happens afterwards. They may simply describe the processes, talking about what humans actually do, and making no attempt to say what humans ought to do. Books on Christian ethics will make more conscious judgments about whether certain actions are right or wrong, and may list the things Christians should do in many different circumstances. But both kinds of writers are nearly always talking about individual decision-making at a particular point. Sometimes the implication is that life is plain sailing, with problems cropping up at intervals, a decision being made, and then life jogging along as before. Nevertheless, the aftermath of making one choice can simply involve more choices. We change the situation and the next issue is already waiting for us. Consequences of decisions taken some time ago are still reverberating round us. Life is usually much more complicated than writers on ethics sometimes suggest.

But like Darren, every now and again we are confronted with the consequences of how we have chosen to live, and we urgently wish there was a way to go back, start again, learn our lessons and make good the damage we have caused.

The most crucial item in a Christian worldview is that God has provided for that urgent wish. The central tenet of Christianity is that Jesus Christ, who is God, became a man and died a human death. His death carried enormous weight and significance, more than any other event in the history of the world. His death and resurrection make it possible for us to start again. Now, this is a book about how to live and not a book about Christian doctrine. The atonement—the way in which Jesus's death on the cross provides for our redemption, salvation and forgiveness—is an enormous subject. Some of you reading this may have many questions about it, but for now we need only to work out its importance in living a good life. For our purposes in this chapter, the immensity of God's love, forgiveness and mercy have huge implications for moral and good living.

There is a way out for Darren, but it may not be easy. We all make mistakes. There are times when all of us are deliberately destructive. More frequently, we can be negligent and thoughtless. The first require-ment for good living is a willingness to acknowledge our errors and wrongdoing. The second is that we are honest. To start again, all the wild cards have to go down on the table. The third is that we genuinely want to put our past behind us and start again—an attitude that we sometimes call repentance.

It is possible to wish we had done things differently, but for the wrong reasons. We can be filled with regret, but mainly because things have gone wrong and we have been found out. All our regrets may only lead us to ensure that we are more careful and secretive next time. Darren just might go home and be contrite enough to engineer a reconciliation with his wife. She probably longs for that, but he may have no intention of changing his ways, or he may be so weak that he is not able to. It is not easy to seek forgiveness. It is not easy to say sorry. It is not easy to be exposed as weak and thoughtless. But seeking the forgiveness of God and then the forgiveness of those who have been harmed is enormously liberating.

Darren's wife has to be able to forgive him. Many people do not find that easy. We sometimes enjoy feeling that we are better than others and that we have acted in an upright way. However much we have been sinned against, we find some crumb of comfort in self-righteousness! Jesus said, 'If someone wants to sue you and take your tunic, let him have your cloak as well. If someone forces you to go one mile, go with him two miles.' At first glance, such teaching seems outrageous, and yet it is this kind of behaviour that is called out of us when we have to forgive someone who has treated us very badly. It may not even seem fair, but then neither does going a second mile.

We make mistakes and go down the wrong road. We realize what we have done and stop. We are honest with ourselves, with God and with those we have affected. We seek forgiveness and want to start again. But there are many situations we cannot change. We cannot undo the past. We have to live with the consequences of what we have done. How will Darren act now? It will take time to regain the trust and love of his wife. It will take time to restore his relationship with his children. Should he change his job? Can he trust himself to stay alone in strange hotels again? Should he admit that he cannot be away from home as he has been in the past without risking his new-found family peace.

Knowing that there is redemption through Jesus Christ, knowing that we can be forgiven and that we can start again, is the core of a Christian worldview. We believe that God has provided a way out and that any and every situation can be redeemed. God can change us. He can heal and restore and his power through his Holy Spirit is available to us. He can heal Darren's addiction to pornography, but it may take time and Darren has to take some action himself. God can overrule the damage that causes many of us to make mistakes. He can soften the effects of bad parenting, of child abuse and neglect. He can restore low self-esteem. He can mitigate the effects of all the various kinds of handicap—physical, mental and emotional—that afflict every human being. He can change communities and even nations, but it can take time. He works through human agencies. He does not redeem us against our will.

This power is available to us as we seek to live good lives, to act rightly and to obey God's laws. Right at the beginning of the Ten Commandments, the Bible makes the same point. The first commandment is usually given as, 'You shall have no other gods beside me.' But those are not the first words of the commandment. It begins, 'I am the Lord your God who brought you out of Egypt, out of the land of slavery.' Before God begins to list the rules by which the Israelites are to live, he reminds them that they are redeemed and forgiven people. These laws are a description of the lifestyle of those who have been saved, rescued, and restored to healthy living by a God who loves and redeems his people and has put them on the right road. He is the God who rescued them from slavery, and in gratitude, love and obedience, they follow the guidelines he has given for their life with him. The commandments are not a list of dos and don'ts that have to be performed in order to satisfy a policeman God. They are not the rules we have to obey in order to get into heaven.

The rules and guidelines, precepts and commands, virtues and principles that we learn from the Bible are not a drudgery of trying to obey a hard taskmaster. They are the way we choose to live because we have been loved and redeemed. They are our obedience in love to a Father who forgives us, picks us up and offers us a fresh start over and over again.

CHAPTER 20

Will it all work out in the end?

Janine had been on a sixth-form field trip to North Dakota. One of the best parts of the trip was the discovery that clothes were so cheap in the States. Janine was going home with a lot of purchases. When it came to filling in the Customs forms, she listed all that she had bought. Never having travelled overseas before, she was a little scared of the consequences of simply putting the clothes and other presents in her bag and ignoring the need to declare them, as many of her friends were doing. At Customs she was asked to pay tax on a proportion of the goods she had bought. She was very indignant. She was convinced that the reward for being honest should be that any payments due should be waived. It took her some minutes to see how illogical her position was.

Many of us have an almost unconscious sense that if we make the effort to do what is right and to be honest, then we should get something in return. There should be some reward. Too often we seem to get no benefit from being good. In fact, sometimes we are aware that we have lost out. We have been honest about our expenses, but the man sitting at the desk next to us has put down a great number of dubious items and has gained a substantial sum. Nobody finds out and he gets away with it. It is not fair.

What kind of a world is this? If it is simply hard work being good and it doesn't seem to make any difference anyway, then what is the point? We want 'good' to win and 'bad' to be punished. We want justice, fairness and the right rewards and punishments. Human beings do not like an arbitrary world. They long for fairness and balance, and they try to find ways to provide this fairness. It simply does not happen in this world, however, and we have to believe that the solution has to lie in the world to come. Justice has to come in another life after death. Some see reincarnation as solving the problem: the reward or the punishment will come in being reincarnated in a higher or lower place in creation. Some visualize the judgment seat of God, where all human beings will have their good and bad deeds weighed in a balance and justice will be meted out according to which scale dips lower.

People are always longing to make sense of the injustice and unfairness of the world. Many of the world's stories are seeking to do this. Homer did it for the Greeks, Virgil for the Romans. Stories like Cinderella, *War and Peace*, and even Tom and Jerry, all to a greater or lesser degree toy with ideas about bad and good. Some of the most graphic and exciting stories have a plot that puts good and evil on opposite sides of the battleground. They encourage us to identify with the good, keep us on tenterhooks as the battle runs its course, and then give us the satisfaction of seeing good win and bad defeated. Everything is put right, the hero gets the princess, and everyone lives happily ever after. Some of the most distressing films in recent years have been those that reflect more accurately the meaninglessness of life for many, and kick us in the teeth by allowing good to be defeated and bad to triumph.

Christians live in the hope that it will all work out in the end. Yet 'hope' is probably the wrong word. It is not the kind of hope that says, 'I hope it rains tomorrow'. The hope that the Bible teaches us is more like the excited anticipation of a party. One day God will sort it all out. One day we will know why things happened the way they did, although we could not understand at the time. One day love will triumph, Jesus will reign and every knee will bow before him. There will be no endless round of reincarnation, no weighing of the balances—all human personal scales are very light on the good side already. Heaven is not for the good but for the forgiven.

However, we saw in the last chapter that the forgiven try to be good, not to earn their way into God's favour, but to please a father who loves them. If I take the right course but seem to be losing out, I know that I will be vindicated, but it may not come until the end of time. With this great hope in us, we can survive the unfairness and injustice. Some of the most passionate lines in the psalms, the hymns of Israel, call out to God in frustration because the wicked prosper and the righteous lose out. The weak are trodden on, the strong become stronger. 'Why have you rejected us for ever, O God?' says one psalm. 'We are given no miraculous signs, no prophets are left, and none of us knows how long this will be.' The Bible faces up to the reality of the unfairness of this world. 'The race is not to the swift or the battle to the strong, nor does food come to the wise or wealth to the brilliant or favour to the learned; but time and chance happen to them all.'

This will not be the case for ever, says the Bible. The day will come when you will see good rewarded and evil destroyed. In the final great vision of the Bible, John, a disciple of Jesus, describes the throne of God, surrounded by a great multitude from every nation, tribe, people and language. 'They serve God day and night... Never again will they hunger; never again will they thirst... And God will wipe away every tear from their eyes.' We do good not because we know we will be rewarded. We do good not because others will praise us. We do good because even though it may be to our loss now, it is our service to the Lord who loves us, and who one day we will meet face to face.

Creation, the fall, redemption and a glorious climax to history—those are the key points in a Christian world view. They undergird our thinking and our working out of our moral behaviour and decision-making.

CHAPTER 21

Growing Christian character

Books about ethics frequently concentrate on the point at which an individual has to decide how to act. At that moment the individual has to decide whether an action is right or wrong, whether the consequences can be foreseen and whether they are good or bad. The books usually add a chapter in which they talk about character and virtues. Way back in the 4th century BC, Aristotle wrote a great deal about virtues, dividing them into moral and intellectual virtues. Moral virtues were developed through habit and intellectual ones by instruction and learning. Humans should develop habits of courage, patience and truthfulness. Aristotle also included magnificence, wittiness and righteous indignation, seeing all these qualities as the middle way between excesses. Wittiness was the middle way between buffoonery and boorishness!

Intellectual virtues included technical skill, scientific knowledge, and judgment. Cultivating these virtues and working at the maturing of a good character leads to wisdom. Wise people will know how to make wise decisions. They will already have in place the tools to assess difficult situations. They will not be caught out by emotion too strong to resist. They will not be hassled into taking a path that they will regret bitterly afterwards. They will, at the least, be far less likely to do these things than their 'foolish' neighbour.

The Bible has a lot to say about wisdom and about what a mature Christian character will be like. In this chapter we will look briefly at the overall biblical themes of virtue and attributes of character that are pleasing to God. Many of these themes are similar to Aristotle's.

The underlying bedrock of biblical ethics is that we should be like God. Children of God should be like their father. The Israelite people of God, as a nation, were meant to embody God-like characteristics in their communal life. The aim of Christian discipleship is to be conformed to the likeness of Christ. We therefore need to ask what the character of God is like. We can look at Jesus' life on earth and seek to follow his example. We should also look at the virtues and traits of character that are recommended in the Bible.

To list and develop all the aspects of the character of God revealed to us in the Bible is a subject for a whole book. If you ask a group of Christians to list some of the ways we can describe God, they usually mention: loving, almighty, sovereign, creating, merciful and faithful. These are all attributes of God that are developed in the Bible. There are so many that we need to pick out some that have a more obvious relevance to our ethical thinking.

God is love. The apostle John says that in one of his letters. The Bible is full of phrases about God and his unfailing love that endures for ever. But we can think of the love of God in rather abstract ways, saying that God loves the world, or in personal ways—'God loves me'. Crucial to the understanding of the love of God is the Christian doctrine of the Trinity. God from the beginning exists in relationship; it is inadequate to have a picture of God as one sovereign creator, who splits into two or three persons when the incarnation, or the coming of the Holy Spirit, demands it. He is, and always was, before the creation of the universe, God in three persons, Father, Son and Holy Spirit, in a complex and mysterious relationship of active, creative love. The love of this relational God is a sacrificial love that goes all the way to the cross for his beloved sons and daughters.

Humans have a great longing for love built into them, from the moment they are born and begin to relate to their mother. Being deprived of love damages us. To follow God and be his obedient child means a lifetime of working out what love means and how to promote it so that those around us are helped to flourish and blossom.

He is a God of abundant generosity. He creates lavishly—thousands of tadpoles, millions of acorns, hundreds of different orchids. We need water, and he pours it down waterfalls, turns it into snowflakes, covers mountain tops with snow. He gives humans the ability to search out and discover, invent and create. He gives us freedom—the ultimate generosity—so that we can choose to serve him. He loves us, but in his generosity he allows us to walk away from him, making a mess of our own lives and those of others. He does not compel. At the end of time he promises us not servanthood, but kingship, sitting down to the banqueting feast of heaven. He is a God of enormous generosity. How do we follow him in that?

He is a God who takes responsibility for all that he has created. He has given us the task of running his world, yet he does not allow us to make such a mess that we would be frustrating his purposes. We do not know how often he rescues us from disaster, how often he stays the hand of evil powers—not so that the world is cocooned in cottonwool, a place where nothing can go wrong and nothing can harm, but so that destruction and evil do not go too far. Even when he gives us this freedom to disobey him and turn away from him, the Bible describes his pain at our waywardness, his patience with us, his willingness to wait for our repentance and conversion.

These are some of the characteristics of God. Sometimes it is when we first become parents ourselves that we gain some of our most revealing insights into the nature of God. When we have to act in love, not compulsion, to allow young adults freedom to make mistakes, weeping over children who go wrong and will not listen to us, that we understand something of God's parenthood. Looking at it from the other side, we are also strengthened by our understanding of the character of God as we seek to act towards our children with love that is shaped by justice and authority.

Jesus did not come to live in our world solely as an example for us. He came to teach; he came to fulfil the Old Testament prophecies about the way God would deal with human sin; he came to die and he came to rise again from death and establish his reign for ever. In one sense we cannot follow his example. He was the sinless Son of God and we are incapable of living as he did. But in the four records we have of his life, we can see the perfect character of God living in a crowded, dirty, cruel and uncomfortable world. There we find clues and pointers to guide us as we seek to know just what human beings should be like.

He showed great patience and love towards individuals of every kind, befriending those who were despised and outcast, touching the unclean, the lepers, debating theology with women, treating children with respect. Even when he had another objective, he would stop and spend time with anyone who accosted him. He taught with authority but he did not force people to believe in him. He did not pull rank and insist that they listened to him. He allowed them to walk away. Maybe one of the most telling characteristics of Jesus is this relinquishing of rank. Paul says that we should do nothing out of selfish ambition or vanity; instead we should have the same attitude that Jesus had, who, 'being in the form of God, did not consider equality with God something to be grasped'. This kind of humility is not the kind that acts like a doormat, but it is willing to allow others to take the higher positions, willing to listen to what others have to say, and does not insist on rank. 'I have set you an example,' Jesus said after he had washed his disciples' dirty feet, 'that you should do as I have done for you.' He sought out the people who were in the most despised and mucky corners of a mucky world. It is very hard for us to do that and stay whole and untainted as he did. We can protect ourselves from some of the most difficult ethical dilemmas by simply never getting involved. But that is not the Christian way.

And much more than being just a mentor and role model, Jesus, through his Spirit, has the power to change us, so that we are being conformed to his likeness. This power comes from someone who knows what it is like to fight human temptations, who knows how difficult it is to do the right thing when hunger and tiredness are overwhelming, who knows the longing to avoid painful and heart-rending situations. We cannot ask for more than that.

The Bible tells us what the fruits, the traits of a Christlike character will be. One passage lists love, joy, peace, patience, kindness, goodness, faithfulness, gentleness and self-control. Some of the other lists involve our community life—servanthood, hospitality, generosity, encouragement, consideration for others' weaknesses, maintaining unity, strict sexual morality, truthfulness, not gossiping, bearing each others' burdens, and forgiving grievances. Paul ends one list of such traits by saying, 'Over all these virtues put on love, which binds them all together in perfect unity.'

Some of these characteristics, these fruits, are harder to cultivate than others. Different people have a natural tendency to one rather than the others. We cannot always wait for them to become our real feelings. We may have to love where we do not feel it. We may have to have self-control when it is almost impossible. We may have to exercise patience with a child, when everything in us wants to box its ears. Some of these traits are not easy in certain situations. Gentleness may not be easy to exercise in some company boardrooms!

Perhaps we can see now how much influence we have as parents. Our children will learn to despise those quieter traits, and admire belligerence, bullying, dominance and status, if that is what our lives and actions are saying.

We seek to follow Jesus Christ throughout our lives, praying to him, reading and absorbing the message of the Bible, growing into mature adult believers within the fellowship of Christians to which we have been called. As we do so we learn wisdom and discernment, so that we are able to bring a Christian mind to bear on all the issues we have to face. We are 'buried with him through baptism into death in order that, just as Christ was raised from the dead through the glory of the Father, we too may live a new life'.

CHAPTER 22

Down to detail

Within the Christian community, we learn to live the Christian way together. We worship together, pray together, we go out to serve the local community, take part in social action, live within our families and do our daily work, building the Kingdom of God. We share what we learn from the Bible with each other, studying, discussing and praying over what we have learnt, on our own and in our fellowship groups. The Bible shows us what a Christian character looks like, tells us the traits and virtues that we should begin to develop, shapes our thinking so that we are no longer conformed to this contemporary world, but have a Christian worldview. It also gives us, in a range of different forms, the rules and principles by which we should live.

Sometimes, working out what exactly the Bible teaches seems to be far harder than we had expected. We have shown already in this book how some of the commands that appear so straightforward on the surface have to be unpacked, and even then we differ on their application to specific situations. We may read a rule and then discover exceptions to it, stories about people who did or did not keep it, verses that appear to contradict. How do we proceed? In this chapter we will look at some of the Ten Commandments, as probably the most familiar list of rules in the Bible.

The Ten Commandments, and the story of how they were given to the children of Israel through Moses, are told twice, once in the book of Exodus (chs. 19—20) and again in the book of Deuteronomy (ch. 5). You may like to look them up before you read any further. I suggest that you read them in the translation you are familiar with, but also find a new version that is different from your usual one. Once upon a time, most people in Britain could recite the Ten Commandments. They were taught at school, at home and at Sunday school. We are not so familiar with them nowadays. A couple of years ago a group of ministers was asked to name them. Many of them could not do so, and those who could not suggested that they were negative and old-fashioned, and that we had moved on from them.

Of course the commandments were given to a particular people at a particular time, and some of the wording reflects their society and culture. The tenth commandment says that we should not covet our neighbour's ox or donkey or anything that belongs to them. But most of us have no trouble in substituting other items for oxen and donkeys.

One writer has given an illuminating introduction to the commandments, explaining their context as laws given to a nation which had just emerged from slavery in Egypt. He suggests that they form a Bill of Rights for a liberated people. Only three months before they were given, the Israelites had been in political, economic, social and spiritual bondage. Each group of commandments gives them back the right to organize their own community life as God's redeemed people.

The first group of commandments, which are about the worship and honouring of God, restored to the people of Israel the proper worship of God after their time of slavery in Egypt, where Pharaoh claimed to be divine and where they were surrounded by the idolatrous statues of Egyptian religion. The Sabbath day of rest restored the dignity of labour to exploited slaves, and reminded them to make sure that the vulnerable, the people at the bottom of the social pile, also rested.

The commandments about family life restored the dignity of Israelite families, whereas in Egypt they had suffered intolerable intrusion into family life, with the threat of genocide when all their boy babies were to be killed. Their legal system was to be restored and freed from corruption and falsehood.

How do we apply these great laws to ourselves? Looking at the outline above, we can see that these laws do not tell us what to do: they tell us what not to do. They provide the outer boundaries that we should not cross. Within them we fill in from the rest of the Bible the kind of lives we should lead. For example, the seventh commandment says that we should not commit adultery. But within that framework of trust, we read all the other passages that describe for us the kind of relationship we should experience within marriage. It is possible to obey the seventh commandment totally, and yet within a marriage to be vicious and destructive, bullying and unloving.

It is not possible to look at all the commandments in this chapter. We will look more closely at three of them, searching out passages from the rest of the Bible that help us to understand how we should obey. This same method can be applied to all of them.

'Honour your father and your mother' is the fifth commandment. This commandment is not addressed to children, although they are of course included in it. It is adults who are being told to honour their parents. Within this kin-based, tribal, agricultural society, the implications of this command were far wider than just making sure parents were well cared for. It underlines the importance of authority and responsibility in society. The parental generation were the ones who were in authority, they were the heads of the extended households of kin and servants. The commandment calls for respect, for listening to older people who have had more experience. It is about maintaining the structures of society by appropriate behaviour from younger to older members. Obeying it contributes to the security and stability of society. As the commandment says, 'Honour them so that you may live long in the land the Lord your God has given you.'

Our children learn to honour us in their turn, because of the way we honour our parents. If we treat our parents with impatience and carelessness, our children may well do the same and the traditional structures of society are weakened. We all need long-term, committed, covenant relationships within which to grow and flourish as adults and to support us in our declining years.

This commandment is not just about fathers; it is not an invitation to perpetual patriarchy. Mothers are to be honoured as well, which has implications for the relationship between men and women in the ruling structures of the society. They are not to be belittled by domestic drudgery.

For many of us, the question is how we obey this commandment in our modern world. We have reconstructed families, with step-parents and grandparents, children living with one birth parent and visiting the other birth parent. We have isolated and mobile nuclear families living far from kin. We have to think through how we honour our parents within these changing structures.

But we can also look further afield within the Bible to see how we should carry out this commandment. We may read the story of Ruth and Naomi, two widows, mother-in-law and daughter-in-law. Ruth demonstrates the wider implications of the commandment as she commits herself to her mother-in-law. We may look at the references to Jesus and his family in the gospels. We see him living with his parents and obeying them through his early years and into his adult life. But when he begins his public ministry, there is a different emphasis. One account describes how his family go to take charge of him, saying that he is out of his mind. Someone tells Jesus that his mother and brothers have come. Jesus replies, 'Who are my mother and my brothers? ... Whoever does God's will is my brother and sister and mother.'

Jesus calls his disciples to leave their families and parents. John and James leave their father and his fishing business to follow Jesus. Jesus seems to be saying that the family is not an overriding principle that should take precedence over everything else. It is more important to do the will of God and follow him. We are not to carry the commandment to honour our parents so far that we let them rule our lives and determine how we are to live. We may have to cut the ties.

If we live in a church community of Christians, but our own parents and grandparents live far away, can we extend this commandment within the fellowship? Should we not seek to incorporate other people's parents into our own family life in the place of our own who may be far away? Then we can obey the commandment in a far wider sense. We can recreate family structures for all those who have no family close by, within the family of faith. Paul, in his first letter to Timothy, tells him to treat older men in the church as fathers and older women as mothers. Jesus said that we should of course honour our own parents, and he told off those who thought of excuses so that they did not have to support their elderly parents. We cannot simply hand over respons-ibility to other people. Paul also tells Timothy that if widows have no one to care for them they should become a church responsibility. If they have their own children, then these children should care for them.

What happens to disobedient children? In one place in the Old Testament, the law describes how parents of a rebellious, stubborn and profligate son should take him to the elders for judgment and that the punishment should be death. However, Jesus tells the story of a son who betrays his obligations to his father, and comes back as the prodigal or profligate son, to be loved, forgiven and reinstated. Paul tells parents that they should not provoke their children. There are obligations of care and respect on both sides.

'Honour your father and mother' and 'Do not commit adultery' are the two commandments that relate to family life. Whole books are written on Christian family and marriage and Christian understandings of sexuality. Issues such as divorce and remarriage, homosexuality, polygamy and singleness, as well as newer issues about infertility treatment, should all have as their outer boundaries these two commandments. And those searching for biblical guidance will also read all the other passages that contribute to a full understanding of these issues, reading the Old Testament in the light of the New. Jesus developed and expanded many of the commandments in his teaching called the Sermon on the Mount. Human sexual love is explored in the Song of Songs. The stories of Bible characters give us insights into both the right and the wrong ways of following the Lord's commands. It is an exciting voyage of discovery.

The commandments not to steal and not to covet also seem quite straightforward, but these too are expanded and developed by the rest of the biblical narrative. We have a tendency to hear them as commands to ourselves as individuals: 'I must not steal; I must not covet.' As long as I don't reach out my hand and take something that is not mine, or long for something that is not mine, then I have kept the commandments. But is this as far as they go?

The book of Deuteronomy, where the Ten Commandments are recorded for the second time, has chapters of instructions that develop each commandment in turn. These are some of the ones that are relevant to the commands about coveting and stealing: 'If you enter your neighbour's vineyard, you may eat all the grapes you want, but do not put any in your basket.' 'Do not charge your brother interest, whether on money or food or anything else that may earn interest. You may charge a foreigner interest, but not a brother... Do not take a pair of millstones—not even the upper one—as security for a debt, because that would be taking a man's livelihood as security... Do not take advantage of a hired man who is poor and needy... Pay him his wages each day before sunset, because he is poor and counting on it... You must have accurate and honest weights and measures.'

These commands were addressed to a community. Much of the law showed not just how individuals, nor just households, should obey the law, but how society as a whole was to demonstrate the holiness and character of God to the surrounding nations.

The commands not to steal and not to covet were translated into a community spirit of care and compassion, especially for the weak and the poor. We have not always read them like this. It has been possible in the past for someone to say, with hand on heart, 'I have totally kept these commandments.' The person speaking, however, might have been a slave-owner in a large mansion in the Southern States of America, or the owner of a mine or factory in Britain that involved a brutal system of economic exploitation. The 16th-century reformer, John Calvin, said that the commandment not to steal covered all sorts of unjust gain at the expense of others. Those of us who live in the richer parts of the world, or even in the richer parts of our own society, need to hear these commandments afresh.

CHAPTER 23

Living in the modern world

In the last chapter we looked at some of the commandments that are included in the great ten, given to the people of God in the Old Testament. We looked at the way we can develop their meaning by seeing how they are worked out in the rest of scripture. The people of Israel who received these commandments lived together in a small nation that sought to follow God's laws in every part of their lives together, social, economic and political, as well as in their families and their individual lives. The Bible records that they were not very successful in this. There is a catalogue of failure, both as a nation and as individuals. They struggled, failed and deliberately went the wrong way in much the same way as we do today.

Today we do not live together as the people of God. Christians live scattered throughout the world in nations which do not seek to do the will of God. It is the Church that now has to fill the role of the Old Testament people of God. Just as Israel was called to demonstrate God's laws and God's morality to the surrounding nations, so we, as groups of Christians, should be seeking to show our neighbours and our societies just what Christian living is like.

The apostle Peter wrote a letter to the small groups of Christians scattered in the towns of Asia Minor in the first century AD, 2000 years ago. The situation was hostile to them in many ways. They attempted to live the Christian way and were misunderstood and falsely accused of various anti-social activities. There were wives with non-Christian husbands, slaves with non-Christian masters, their neighbours were pagans and the local authorities were suspicious of them.

Peter tells them to build up their Christian community so that they can encourage and support each other. He tells them to love each other intensely from the heart, and to remember that they are the people of God, chosen, loved, forgiven, with a joy and a hope that nothing can destroy, not even ill-treatment and persecution. 'Rid yourselves,' says Peter, 'of all spite, deceit, hypocrisy, envy and carping criticism' (NJB).

Peter refers back to the Old Testament to guide them in their day-to-day living. He reminds them of a verse in Leviticus we have already referred to. He says to them, 'As obedient children, be yourselves holy in all your activity, after the model of the Holy One who calls us, since the scripture says, "Be holy, for I am holy."'

The main thrust of what Peter says is that the Christians should imitate Jesus, particularly imitating the way he behaved when he was on trial before his execution. Peter is reminding the wives, slaves and other Christians in those small churches that they could do very little about the unjust situations they were caught up in. They could not influence how their neighbours and local authorities treated them. Slaves with unjust masters had no rights, no way to get out of slavery. To try to escape would mean terrible retribution. They had to endure. Peter tells them to do good even though they may be misunderstood and falsely accused of wrongdoing. He tells them to live good lives that can be seen, and not to talk back or argue. He tells them to restrain their tongues, to be peacemakers, not to return evil for evil, echoing the words of Jesus.

But above all, he tells them to remember how Jesus acted and follow his example. He had done nothing wrong and had spoken no deceit. He was insulted and did not retaliate with insults. When he was suffering he made no threats but put his trust in God. The emphasis in this letter is on endurance, on being humble and self-effacing; on being a loving and supportive community which helps its members to take the injustices and ill-treatment of the world, and does not return evil for evil, does not retaliate.

We sometimes need to be reminded that aggressiveness, fighting for one's rights, making sure that others know they are wrong, is not always the best way to be moral and good. But at the same time we have to remember that Peter's world was very different from ours. It was not a democracy; many people, including wives and slaves, had few rights, and endurance was the only option open to them. Today we do have the means to fight injustice. We are called to build up those who are oppressed so that they can seek redress. We should be seeking ways to end injustice and exploitation. We may even have to face the uncomfortable fact that we are part of unjust structures ourselves. We may be those in control, with power in society, unlike the Christians to whom Peter was writing.

However, Christian communities are still called to build loving and supportive relationships that help us all as individuals to live the good life. In addition we are called singly and together to bring the Kingdom of God, that is, the reign of God, into every part of the world around us. We are going to have to get involved in what is going on in our societies. We cannot withdraw without being disobedient. We need to use our influence in ways that were not possible for most of those early Christians.

We need to be involved in questions of social welfare, homelessness and low pay; medical ethics, euthanasia, abortion and fertility treatment; in scientific and technological advance; in economic questions about world trade and Third World debt; in environmental questions about the use of resources and the destruction of the natural world; in business ethics; in human rights, the problem of refugees and the role of the United Nations. All these are legitimate moral and ethical concerns for the Christian Church. But how on earth do we manage to do all that?

First, we work together. In our Christian communities there will be those who can take on, as their special responsibility, the role of resource person—the one who has the information and helps us all, when it becomes important, to think and act on the issues. We may need to take action, perhaps in small groups at local and national level. We may be called to join organizations and pressure groups and to bring their concerns to the church for prayer and information.

We are called to be salt and light. That is what Jesus said we should be—the salt that brings flavour and without which things start to go bad; and the light that shows up the world for what it is, an amazing mix of good and bad, in need of the redeeming power of Jesus in every part. We are his servants. He works through us. We are called to live a good life so that others may come to the light and find him for themselves.

This has been a wide-ranging sketch of the ingredients of Christian ethics, the way Christians are called to live. It is not a book that tells you what to do, but is intended to be a book that helps you to think things through. Various individual dilemmas have been included. It would be possible to go back to work out how a group of Christians might advise those individuals. We would find that they might not always agree. There are difficult areas where the choices do seem to be very hard to make, but the essential ingredients are always the same. We need to train ourselves to have a Christian mind that can distinguish between the rules and attitudes that come from our fallen world, and those that come from God, even though they may often overlap. We need to know our Bibles so that our minds already have a Christian shape to their thinking. Above all, we need to escape from our isolation as individuals and be humble enough to pray and think together with other Christians.

We walk the walk of the redeemed. We have found the right road and we are therefore free. We have a guaranteed hope that it will all work out in the end. We make mistakes, we may even find that we have deliberately done something that we knew was wrong. Always, though, we can find the grace, mercy and forgiveness of God to set us on our feet again as we seek to follow the way of life.

Books to read

BOOKS THAT LOOK AT ISSUES AND DILEMMAS

John Stott, *Issues facing Christians Today: new perspectives on social and moral dilemmas* (Marshall Pickering, 1990 revised edition with study guide)

Richard Higginson, *Dilemmas: a Christian approach to decision making*, (Hodder & Stoughton, 1988)

David Cook, *Dilemmas of Life* (IVP, 1990)

Lewis Smedes, *Mere Morality: how do we make decisions on the things that matter most* (Lion, 1983)

BOOKS THAT REFLECT ON LIVING A GOOD LIFE

Nigel Biggar, *The Good Life: reflections on what we value today* (SPCK, 1997)

David Ford, *The Shape of Living* (Fount, 1997)

OTHER USEFUL BOOKS

William Raeper and Linda Smith, *A Beginner's Guide to Ideas* (Lion, 1991)
A useful and simple introduction to philosophy and ideas in general.

David Cook, *Living in the Kingdom: the ethics of Jesus* (Hodder & Stoughton, 1992)

Mary Stewart van Leeuwen, *Gender and Grace: women and men in a changing world* (IVP, 1990)
An examination of the raising of small children and the influence it has on male and female attitudes in later life. Parts of chapter 4 in this book ('The Importance of Parenting') touch on the material in *Gender and Grace*.

Anton Baumohl, *Making Adult Disciples: learning and teaching in the local church* (Scripture Union, 1984)
The author looks at how we could be learning and growing together in the local fellowship.

Malcolm Goldsmith and Martin Wharton, *Knowing Me, Knowing You: exploring personality type and temperament* (SPCK, 1993)
An examination of personality and ways of assessing our differences, briefly covered in chapter 5 of this book ('Different sorts of people').

Christopher Wright, *The New
International Biblical Commentary:
Deuteronomy* (Paternoster, 1996)
This is a recent commentary on
Deuteronomy where the second
recording of the Ten Commandments
occurs. The approach of this
commentator is mentioned in chapter 22
('Down to detail').

Francis Bridger, *Celebrating the Family*
(Grove Ethical Studies 99a, 1995)
An interesting case study and example of
how changes in the modern world
influence attitudes to morality and ethics
even within the Church.

Gordon D. Fee and Douglas Stuart, *How
to Read the Bible for All Its Worth*
(Scripture Union, 1994)
Besides being possibly the best and most
stimulating introduction to reading the
Bible with understanding, there is a very
useful chapter on reading the Old
Testament Law.

Rob Warner, *The Ten Commandments and
the Decline of the West* (Kingsway, 1997)
A wide-ranging examination of moral
attitudes today based on each of the
Ten Commandments.

Colin Brown, *A Crash Course in Christian
Ethics* (Hodder & Stoughton, 1998)
A lively and accessible guide to the basics
of ethics in general and Christian ethics
in particular.

Margaret Killingray and Jo Bailey Wells,
Using the Ten Commandments (Grove
Biblical B17, Grove Books Ltd, 2000)

Day by Day with God

Margaret Killingray is a regular contributor to *Day by Day with God*, the regular Bible reading notes published jointly by BRF and Christina Press. *Day by Day with God* provides daily notes, including a short printed Bible passage, which explains and applies God's word, written by women who have themselves found the Bible an invaluable guide and encouragement. Whether life for you is over-busy, or seems empty, you will be inspired and encouraged as you try to make sense of life and God's purposes for you each day.

The following extract of readings by Margaret Killingray on 'The Ten Commandments' first appeared in the January–April 2001 issue of *Day by Day with God*.

Exodus 20:1–17(NIV)

The Ten Commandments

And God spoke all these words.

Before starting this new series in which we will look at the Ten Commandments, stop and think for a minute. How many of them can you remember without looking them up? Did you know that Moses brought them down to the people of Israel from a mountain-top meeting with God, only three months after they had left a life of slavery in Egypt? It might be an interesting exercise to ask some of the people you know whether they can recall any of the ten. In a survey a couple of years ago, even ministers found it hard to name them all!

Do read through chapter 20 of Exodus, if you can. As you read and are perhaps reminded again of what the commandments say, what is your reaction to them? Does anything new or surprising strike you about them? God spoke these words to the people of Israel over thirty centuries ago. He wanted them to hear, learn, understand and obey. This is the way he wanted them to live. But what about us?

The laws given to the people of Israel in the Old Testament cannot often be applied as they are, directly to our own lives as Christians in Christian fellowships. We need to look at what other parts of the Bible say in explaining them, especially at the words of Jesus. Do you expect them to challenge you, to make you think again about the way you live? Or are you thinking that there are a lot of other parts of the Bible you would rather read? Getting to grips with the Old Testament laws is a challenge that can be very rewarding, and a good place to start is with these commands.

I want to walk your way every day of my life. These words may be just the ones you want to speak to me each day, Lord. Help me to use my mind and heart to listen.

MK

Exodus 19:1–6, 16–19 (NIV)

A solemn covenant

Now if you obey me fully and keep my covenant, then out of all nations you will be my treasured possession.

Chapter 19 describes a momentous and terrifying meeting with God. Three months ago the people of Israel had been slaves in Egypt. During those months they had been led by Moses out of a life of ill-treatment and slave labour, seeing many miracles as God delivered them. Now they stand in the desert, before the mountain we call Sinai, waiting to hear what God through Moses will say to them.

We don't experience many solemn moments like this. Signing on to join the army might be such a moment, when you sign the dotted line and promise to obey, whatever happens, keep all the rules, and accept the possibility of hardship, injury and death. But this covenant between God and his people is also surprisingly like a marriage. God reminds them that they now know what he is like; how he has rescued them, saved them from slavery, carried them on 'eagles' wings' (19:4), that they will be treasured by him, that he has chosen them out of all other nations to be his special people.

Committing ourselves to a covenant relationship with Jesus and promising to follow him for the rest of our lives in a way echoes the solemnity of signing a contract with the army, *and* making marriage promises. We do not know what battles we may have to fight, but we are his chosen and beloved bride and because we love him we will obey and follow.

These are not laws to be obeyed to win the love and approval of God. He has already loved and saved his people; these are to be obeyed out of love and commitment.

Nothing we can do (even keeping these Ten Command-ments) can make him love us more, and nothing we can do (even breaking them all) can make him love us less. His un-deserved loving kindness that we call grace overwhelms us and in response we will do what pleases him.

MK

Exodus 20:1–3; Colossians 1:15–23 (GNB)

No other gods

He is the firstborn Son, who was raised from death, in order that he alone might have the first place in all things. For it was by God's own decision that the Son has in himself the full nature of God.

'I am the Lord your God. You shall have no other gods before me.' It is almost as if God is saying, 'I will reveal myself to you and then you will love and worship me and me alone.' Human beings cannot really know God or find out anything about him unless he shows himself to us. We can perhaps guess that he is mighty and creative by looking at the world around us. But we cannot know his love, his gentleness, his grace, mercy and forgiveness, his patience with us, his fatherhood, unless he tells us. The people of Israel knew God's love and care as he brought them out of slavery, but we know Jesus, the Son who has in himself the full nature of God.

This is the most amazing truth there is—the God who made the universe, who created everything we know, who made me and you, is shown to us in the man, Jesus Christ. We can read his words, listen to what he did, and we can fall in love with him, a man who knows what it is like to be human, and at the same time is the Lord God almighty, the creator. 'You shall have no other gods but me' is no longer the thunder on the mountain, but an invitation to a relationship as exclusive as the best of marriages, and as loving and intimate. We cannot betray him, turn to anyone or anything else because we are lost in love and adoration for the one who has loved us all the way to death.

I love you, Jesus. I will serve you and no other, for you are my God and there are no other gods.

MK

Exodus 20:4–6; Romans 1:21, 25 (NIV)

Do not make idols

Although they knew God, they neither glorified him as God nor gave thanks to him… They exchanged the truth of God for a lie, and worshipped and served created things rather than the Creator.

Paul's description of idolatry from his letter to the Romans helps us to make sense of one of the more difficult commandments. Of course we don't make idols—we have seen pictures on television of people bowing down to statues and carvings and we know we don't do that. But are there other ways to worship idols? There is a lot about idolatry in the Bible and mostly God is speaking to those who already know him, but still honour, or even worship, things that are not God. Are there things that are so important that we would serve them rather than God?

I have known someone who was so obsessed with having a clean and tidy house that she actually resented it when her family took books off the shelves, read the paper and left it on the coffee table, disturbed the fruit bowl by eating an apple or had a wonderful time with messy games. She had made the shell of their lives more important than their living. Can we do this with God? Valuing the way things are done in church rather than the worship itself? Following a church leader rather than the God he is teaching us about? Knowing God, but not caring to find out more about him? Nor joining with other believers in worship and prayer? Are we serving created things, even our own comfort, rather than the creator? Is God hidden from us by all the busyness, obsessions and little importances that we value so much?

It is very hard to see our own 'idols'. Sometimes it is only as we share and pray with a few trusted friends that we begin to see where we are not putting God first.

MK

Hebrews 10:26–31 (NIV)

Do not misuse the name of the Lord

How much more severely do you think those deserve to be
punished who have trampled the Son of God under foot, who have
treated as an unholy thing the blood of the covenant that sanctified
him, and who have insulted the Spirit of grace?

I work in central London, so every Christmas I watch the big stores decorate their windows, and see the lights of Oxford Street come on. We all grumble about aspects of Christmas, the commercialism, the encouragement to buy, especially expensive presents for children. We can see that much of the razzmatazz of Christmas hides and distorts the real meaning of God becoming a baby human being and then experiencing human life with all its hardships and troubles. But what about my grandson's infant school nativity play in which he played the part of a snowflake and the main storyline involved a lost kitten, whose mother searched everywhere and then in the end found her kitten beside the manger? Does that distort the real meaning of Christmas?

The trouble is that I am beginning to think that this command is not about casual 'building site' blasphemy, however distasteful that may be. It is about believers who know the *name* of God (that is, they know him personally and understand his character), who then misuse his name, distort the truth about him, make belief in God and even God himself sound trivial. Perhaps our songs of worship are sometimes just too light and casual. Sometimes we sell Jesus to people as if he is a new kind of comfort blanket that will make them feel better. Read the verse from Hebrews at the top of the page again. How often do our church services convey the awesomeness of God, his splendour, his consuming fire? Do we misuse his name?

Name him, Christians, name him, with love strong as death,
but with awe and wonder, and with bated breath;
he is God the saviour, he is Christ the Lord,
ever to be worshipped, trusted and adored.
CAROLINE M. NOEL (1817–77)

MK

Matthew 12:1–13 (NIV)

Remember the sabbath day

Looking for a reason to accuse Jesus, they asked him, 'Is it lawful to heal on the sabbath?' He said to them, 'If any of you has a sheep and it falls into a pit on the sabbath, will you not take hold of it and lift it out?'

Jesus had problems with people who remembered the sabbath day by keeping a great number of rules, even if that meant being unkind and unloving. Today most of us have problems with making one day in seven any different from all the rest! These are the kinds of changes in society that make knowing how to keep some of the commandments very difficult.

The command suggests that there should be a rhythm about work; that regularly we should stop, have a rest and some re-creation, take a breath before we start again. Many people are under such pressure and stress at work that this would seem to be very good advice. The command also suggests that we, particularly if we are employers, should take some responsibility for those around us, who won't be able to have some rest unless we allow them to.

To keep this command may require us to take stock of how our lives work out at the moment. Do you give enough time for simply sitting around, playing with the children, going for walks with friends? When someone gets a video to watch, do you sit down and watch it with them, or do you take the opportunity to tidy up, wash up, clear up?

But the sabbath commandment is not just about rest, it is also about keeping some time holy. We may not be able to rest on Sunday, the 'new' sabbath, which replaced the Jewish Saturday sabbath, or keep it holy in the ways we would like, but we can still build into our lives and the lives of those around us time to reflect, time to rest and time to look back and above all time with God.

Be honest with yourself: do you manage to make time to rest, reflect and pray?
MK

Mark 3:31–35 (NIV)

Honour your father and mother

'Who are my mother and my brothers? … Whoever does God's will is my brother and sister and mother.'

A rather successful church youth group had attracted a number of young people from non-churchgoing homes. One girl of 15 was in some distress because her parents had forbidden her to go to the group or to church. They regarded it as some kind of sect or cult, brainwashing the young and teaching them a lot of fairy tales. Should she withdraw and do what they ask, or does she have the right to disobey?

This command is not addressed to children—all of the command-ments were addressed to adults, although, of course, children were included in the family and would be taught these commands by their parents. But it is about honouring and respecting our parents.

In the agricultural kin-based society of the Old Testament, parents, particularly fathers, controlled work, provided housing, educated and trained and arranged marriages for their children. So sometimes the command has been extended to include anyone in authority, in school, in the workplace, in government. We should always honour those 'above' us. But does this mean we should always do what they say and obey them?

In this story from Mark's Gospel, Jesus' mother comes to talk to him. It is clear from other passages that she does not understand his mission. He does not respond to her, but says that the family of faith, the fellowship of those who are disciples, is a closer relationship in some ways than our close family. Obeying God may mean sometimes that although we may still respect our parents, or others in authority, we may have to disobey them.

Honouring our parents means keeping in touch, including them in our lives, making sure they are looked after as they get older. It does not mean agreeing with them or even bringing up our children in the way they brought us up. We have to provide our children with the freedom to honour and respect us, but also sometimes to go their own way.

MK

Matthew 5:21–24 (NIV)

Do not murder

'You have heard that it was said to the people long ago, "Do not murder, and anyone who murders will be subject to judgment." But I tell you that anyone who is angry with a brother or sister will be subject to judgment.'

Yesterday a friend in great distress told me that her son-in-law had left her daughter and their two small children for someone else. Her greatest emotion was one of enormous anger. How could anyone cause their own children such distress and misery and possibly spoil their chances of living a fulfilled and happy life? She wanted to express her anger in words and, if she had been stronger, in blows. Is that the kind of anger Jesus is talking about?

I knew two sisters once: the older one had a good job, was married with successful children; the younger one had never found a job she enjoyed and was always looking for something new. She was consumed with anger because she felt somehow that her sister's good fortune was unfair. This anger had spoilt her life. How far is that the kind of anger Jesus is talking about?

This command raises issues about killing human beings—in war, for example, or judicially by capital punishment—but it also requires us to look at our own lives and ask whether the Lord is pointing out something we should be dealing with. How much anger is there in you? Is it 'righteous' anger about a real injustice? Then maybe you should find out more about the injustice and even take some action. Is it anger against someone else that is eating your heart? Then you may need to confess and forgive. Are you aware of someone else's anger against you? Then again you may need to sort it out with them, even if you feel they are being unfair.

Anger can destroy us and be a form of murder. Or, in love, it can galvanize us into action to change ourselves and the situation.

Dear Lord, help me to deal properly with any anger in my life.

MK

Matthew 5:27–30 (NIV)

Do not commit adultery

I tell you that anyone who looks at a woman lustfully has already committed adultery with her in his heart. If your right eye causes you to sin, gouge it out and throw it away.

Jesus extends the meaning of this commandment to include sexual longing for someone who is not ours. Watch one evening of television and count how many people are in sexual relationships with someone who is not theirs, let alone just looking and longing. It is a very popular plot for all kinds of drama.

I expect that many of the people reading these notes have been affected in some way by the betrayal and breaking of trust that comes with adultery. There are those who spend much of their lives with bitter regrets about an action that now seems so unimportant and brief, but has brought consequences, spoiling the lives of the people they really love—partners, parents, children, friends. Others may be in a marriage that is difficult and loveless. The temptation to find love elsewhere can be enormous.

Verses 29 and 30 in our reading are very strong language and very challenging. They are a measure of the catastrophic seriousness of adultery. Jesus is using graphic picture language to tell us we should avoid temptation at all cost; some have to fight this battle over alcohol, and some with sex and 'romance'. If we have a weakness, we cannot just do what others do; we have a special battle of our own.

But the gospel of Jesus is about repentance and forgiveness. There is no situation that cannot receive the balm of his love and grace. We all live with limits, handicaps, that we wish were not there; physical disability, failing exams, not being able to have our own children, never finding the right person to marry, spoiling the relationship that really mattered. In Jesus we learn to forgive and accept forgiveness, put things right as far as we can, accept the place and relationships we are in, and live to the full for him, within the limits that have been set for us.

MK

Mark 10:17–22 (NIV)

Do not steal

'One thing you lack,' [Jesus] said. 'Go, sell everything you have and give to the poor, and you will have treasure in heaven. Then come, follow me.'

An attractive, rich young man comes to Jesus. He wants to be the very best for God and earn his place in heaven and asks Jesus how he should do this. Jesus suggests to him that he already knows the commandments and reminds him of some of them. The young man claims that he has kept them since he was a boy. The story then says that Jesus looked at him and loved him, but also gave him the instructions in our verse. Why did he add something so radical to the commandments?

One of the commandments Jesus listed was 'Do not steal'. The young man was convinced that he had never stolen. But if he was rich in a poor society, could that be wholly true? What is stealing? Does it simply mean taking something that does not belong to us or can we steal in other ways?

There were devout Christians who were slave-owners in the eighteenth century. They would say that they never stole anything. But they took away people's lives, freedom, choices, right to education, to paid employment, to stable family life. Wasn't that stealing? The rich young man who came to Jesus was rich in a poor land, where many were close to starving and widows were often destitute. Are there other ways we can steal, apart from simply taking something with someone else's name on it?

The rich have to ask themselves some very serious questions about what it means not to steal. The commandments are for the community of God's people, not just for the secret conscience of the individual and maybe we are bound not just to keep them, but to make sure that we do not make it more difficult for others to keep them.

The other side of stealing is generosity. Help me, Lord, not to worry about who steals from me, but to be generous with what you have given me.

MK

Leviticus 19:14–18 (NIV)

Do not give false testimony

Do not pervert justice; do not show partiality to the poor or favouritism to the great, but judge your neighbour fairly. Do not go about spreading slander.

What happens when law breaks down, when you cannot trust witnesses, when the police plant evidence to get false convictions, when neighbours can covertly accuse each other to the secret police and have whole families imprisoned? Over the past ten years we have seen on the news terrible cases of injustice and false imprisonment. This commandment is about honesty in the courts; it is about perjury and false testimony.

Some people have suggested that the command is simply telling us not to lie. But I don't think it is as general as that. It is about saying things that hurt others, especially in the area of legal and judicial matters. There are many areas of life that come under this microscope: income tax returns, trade descriptions, secondhand car selling, political manifestos, advertising. If enough people give 'false testimony' in these areas, the judicial system and trade and finance, then the fabric of society begins to come apart around us. Being honest makes society work better, and brings comfort and well-being to our fellow citizens.

But for most of us the way in which we are most likely to disobey this commandment is in gossiping and slandering others. We repeat half-truths and rumours, or facts that are true but should not be repeated, and we too destroy reputations and damage relationships.

MK

Luke 12:22–34 (NIV)

Do not covet

'Do not set your heart on what you will eat or drink; do not worry about it… your Father knows that you need them. But seek his kingdom, and these things will be given to you as well.'

This is a commandment about our feelings and attitudes rather than our actions. Exodus 20:17 tells us not to wish we had our neighbour's belongings. Jesus tells us not to worry about what we will eat, or what we will wear. Human beings can waste their precious lives, hoarding and scheming, worrying and coveting.

It is perfectly reasonable to admire and appreciate things that belong to others, whether it is a lovely garden, a beautiful singing voice, or even success and achievement. We can usually tell when such admiration has turned into covetousness that begins to poison a relationship.

There are examples in the Bible of the terrible consequences of uncontrolled coveting. King Ahab wanted Naboth's vineyard and he ended up breaking commandments five, six, eight and nine. King David coveted Bathsheba, another man's wife. He broke commandments six, seven and eight. By breaking those, they were, of course, breaking the first—their commitment to worship and serve the Lord their God.

It is hard sometimes to live with little, next to people who have a lot. But this law reminds us that we must not let our cravings master us, that we are not entitled to possess everything we want, and that we are called to give up status and the admiration of others, not to seek it. Jesus tells us that if only we change the way we think, change our priorities, then our worrying and coveting will fade. There is an old chorus that goes,

Count your blessings, name them one by one,
Count your blessings, see what God has done.
Count your blessings, name them one by one
And it will surprise you what the Lord has done.

Are you able to change the way you count? It may surprise you. Seek his kingdom first and all these (other) things will be yours as well.

MK

141

Matthew 22:34–40 (NIV)

The two greatest commandments

'Love the Lord your God with all your heart and with all your soul and with all your mind... Love your neighbour as yourself.'

Some experts in the law were disturbed by Jesus' teaching. He seemed to undermine the law or develop it further, as we saw in the commands about murder and adultery. He suggested that they misunderstood some of the laws, particularly the one about keeping the sabbath day. So they set out to test Jesus, asking him to name the greatest commandment in the law. In reply, Jesus did not name any of the Ten Commandments, not even the first one. He took two verses from other parts of the Old Testament; one about loving God, from Deuteronomy 6:4–5, and the other about loving neighbours, from Leviticus 19:18.

Jesus put love at the centre of being good; love at the centre of doing right; love as more important than duty. God is not an exasperated headmaster insisting on petty rules. He is not an angry father who sets down laws that we cannot obey and then punishes us. He is not demanding that we fulfil a list of conditions before he will let us into his heaven. These are not the steps we have to climb in order to find salvation. And yet many of the things people say about God and about Christian standards sound as if this is how they understand them.

Jesus says the first command is that we love God passionately, intelligently, deliberately, with our whole being. And we love him like that because Jesus has shown us what his love is like, the love that searched for us, found us, died for us and saved us, long before we even began to understand what loving meant. Safe and secure in that love, we then begin the magnificent adventure of loving our neighbours as ourselves. And who is our neighbour? Jesus answered that one too in the story of the good Samaritan. Everyone is our neighbour, and those we despise and find hard to love may be more loving neighbours than we are.

MK

Psalm 139:23–24 (NIV)

Search, test, lead

Search me, O God, and know my heart; test me and know my anxious thoughts. See if there is any offensive way in me, and lead me in the way everlasting.

Love the Lord your God:

- Am I committed to him alone for the rest of my life?
- Is there anything else more important to me than my faith in Jesus?
- Do I deny him or use his name flippantly or trivially?
- Do I make time to be with him and pray to him?

Love your neighbour:

- Do I build honour and respect as well as love into my family relationships?
- Do I allow anger to drive me?
- Do I take risks with my marriage, or with the marriages of others?
- Am I keeping what I have even though others are in need?
- Have I damaged other people's lives by gossip?
- Am I honest in business and financial matters?
- Do I long for things that belong to others?

Thanks be to you, O Lord Jesus Christ, for all the benefits which you have given me, for all the pains and insults you have borne for me. O most merciful Redeemer, friend and brother, may I know you more clearly, love you more dearly and follow you more nearly day by day, now and for ever more. Amen.
RICHARD OF CHICHESTER

MK

Day by Day with God is published three times a year in January, May and September. The notes are available from your local Christian bookshop, on subscription direct from BRF (telephone 01865 319700), or via BRF's website: www.brf.org.uk